I0616275

Healing Possibilities

(365 Divine Tools to Consider)

Dr. Omar Reda

Copyright © 2025 by Dr. Omar Reda.

All rights reserved. No part of this publication may be reproduced, distributed, or transmitted in any form or by any means—including photocopying, recording, or other electronic or mechanical methods—without the prior written permission of the publisher, except as permitted by U.S. copyright law.

Cover design by zaRNic

ISBN: 979-8-218-61018-0

"Amazing are the affairs of the believer!

For there is good in every matter concerning him. And this is the case with no one except the believer. If something delightful happens to him, he is thankful, and that is good for him. And if he is afflicted with hardship and bears it with patience that too is good for him".

The Holy Prophet Muhammad (Peace Be Upon Him)

DEDICATION AND ACKNOWLEDGEMENT

This book is a labor of love.

I dedicate it to my beloved family, my parents, my wife, and my three daughters, who have always been my anchor and moral compass. Your love is what keeps me going.

I am grateful for the overwhelming support I have received from many individuals, teams, and organizations, especially from my mentor, Imam Mamadou Toure. I admire your deep insights, and your guidance and tenderness.

I write extensively here about the beloved Prophet Muhammad (PBUH), who endured so much out of his love for us, and whose heart broke whenever he saw his Ummah in distress. It is my hope that this book, by guiding readers toward healing tools from the Quran and Sunnah, may bring some comfort to the heart of the Prophet.

O my beloved, Prophet of Allah, there is nothing I long for more than to be among your neighbors in Paradise.

I am grateful for the English translation of the Quran available online through this free source:

https://quran.com/en.

Finally, this writing is a gift to all trauma survivors around the world, who often find themselves navigating the confusing path of trauma recovery alone. I admire your courage and pray that you find peace and healing soon.

When things seem dark and desperate, remember that Allah has promised ease: **"Is the morning not near?" (Chapter 11, Verse 81)**.

PREFACE

The word of God is unlike any other. It is a creative, restorative, and transformative utterance of exceptional insight.

One of the places where humanity comes into contact with the word of its Creator is the Holy Quran, which, in a beautiful Verse, describes itself as a **"Cure for what is in the hearts" (Chapter 10, Verse 57)**. "What is", is understood here to be a reference to all the diseases that can plague the heart of man: envy, jealousy, hate, but also low sense of self, emotional pain, sorrow, and deep despair, along with all of their personal and interpersonal consequences.

Allah created everything for man and created man for Himself. Among the main creations of Allah are the following three categories: angels, animals, and humans.

Angels are created in a state of ready-made perfection and cannot grow into a higher version of the self. Allah says of them in the Quran, **"Who never disobey whatever Allah orders - always doing as commanded" (Chapter 66, Verse 6)**.

Animals do not have the capacity to think. Instinct is what drives their functions.

Only humans have the capacity and the ability to grow into a higher, more noble, and more elevated version of the self. They do so by overcoming and transcending all of the limitations, obstacles, and impediments that stunt their growth and block their path upward. In short, man rises and elevates the self by first and foremost healing from all the sorrows, pains, and sufferings that are summarized in one dreadful word: trauma.

This book by Dr. Omar Reda gathers 365 Verses of healing from the Quran. As such, Dr. Reda has offered a great service to humanity, because man cannot grow, cannot "become", without healing, and every single human being carries within himself or herself emotional and psychological wounds in need of healing.

These Verses from the Quran, carefully selected by Dr. Reda, comfort our hearts and touch our souls. Each and every one of them is a faithful companion on our journey towards healing, the destination of which is a human being who is whole, centered, at peace with themselves, and ready to serve humanity in the best way possible.

Healing Possibilities is both a path and a promise. It opens for us a path to self-healing through the word of Allah, while at the same time promises that the lessons our trauma holds can be the very sources whereby we gain deep insights into ourselves and our world, and that knowledge will lift us towards the boundless possibilities of the human spirit.

When we know better, we do better; and when we do better, over time, we become better.

Our past trauma, when healed through the sanctified Verses contained in this book, can be the source of our transformation for the better.

This is one of the profound lessons that the 13th century poet Rumi teaches us through one of his most famously quoted short poems:

"I said: What about my eyes?

He said: Keep them on the road.

I said: What about my passion?

He said: Keep it burning.

I said: What about my heart?

He said: Tell me what you hold inside.

I said: Pain and sorrow.

He said: Stay with it. The wound is the place where the light enters you".

Imam Mamadou Toure

Masters degree of Comparative Religion from the Sorbonne University, Paris, France

Senior Imam at Bilal Masjid Association in Beaverton, Oregon, USA

INTRODUCTION

One of the most beautiful and powerful things about the Holy Quran, besides it being the final sacred text and the exact word of God, is the fact that it is also an open invitation to all of mankind to reflect and ponder upon the many miracles contained within.

It is amazing how many new insights and how much wisdom one gains each time they go through the Quran.

The Quran is Allah's open invitation to the whole "community of humanity" to get to know Him.

Allah holds all of His creation sacred, not only "the believers". At the center of the Quranic discourse is the human being.

This universal dimension is heavily emphasized in the Quran. For example, in **Chapter 21, Verse 92**, you hear Allah's voice speaking to His Prophets: **"Indeed, this religion of yours is only one religion, and I am your Lord, so worship Me alone"**.

In **Chapter 17, Verse 70**, He states that, **"Indeed, We have dignified the children of Adam"**, and in **Chapter 95, Verse 4**, He declares that **"Indeed, We created humans in the best form"**.

The Quran also states that man has all that he needs: the potential and the capacity to not only heal himself, but to also be a source of healing for everyone and everything around him.

This writing is a modest attempt at looking at the Holy Book from the lens of trauma.

What inspired me to start this project was coming across **Chapter 6, Verse 38** and hearing Allah saying that, **"We have left nothing out of the Record"**. It made me wonder if healing trauma was included in the Quran, and indeed it was.

Chapter 106, Verse 4 points out that if we lack basic needs, we may not be able to perform the role our Creator has entrusted us with, which is to serve His creation and to make the world a better place.

When man nurses his wounds, he becomes better able to elevate to the status of a healer. It is true that hurt people can repeat the cycles of hurt, but it is also true that healed people can become healers.

Healing, therefore, is not only a possibility, it is a responsibility. Imagine a world where all of us are healed and empowered to operate at our best. That is what Allah expects from us, and that is exactly why He shares countless Divine healing tools in His final book.

The Verses of the Quran, I believe, are **Allah's love letters** to us.

DISCLAIMER

While keeping in mind that, as one of Allah's creation, I will never be able to fathom the infinite Divine wisdom of my Creator, I hope to share some of the tools and skills found in the Quran that can help people who have been through difficult tests, trials, tribulations, and traumatic experiences find much-needed meaning, closure, healing, and peace of mind and soul. It is only through faith in the Merciful and Loving Lord that the human heart finds true mending, tranquility, and comfort.

I share multiple insights from the Quran and from the stories of the noble Prophets, compiling an impressive kit of 365 tools that I hope you will find helpful on your recovery journey.

There is much more to Allah's remedies than what can be included in a single book. You will likely collect a completely different set of tools when you do your own reflection. My hope is that this modest contribution serves as an invitation for more meaningful research and, eventually, more impactful work in this important field of faith-based healing—a sacred space that is usually overlooked.

Given the tender loving care that Allah shows toward His creation, sending His final Prophet Muhammad (PBUH) with the final message of Islam, it is no wonder that the Quran is considered the ultimate, comprehensive, and never-ending source of **Guidance and Healing**.

Healing is a journey, not a destination. Embark on your healing journey with sincerity, excellence, and grace in mind. Go through this book at your own pace, and pause as you see fit. I recommend that you take frequent breaks to ground yourself through mindfulness, meditation, meaningful human connections, or whatever helps you live in the present moment before continuing to read. I also invite you to apply the tools in practical ways—first with colleagues you trust—so you can master them when working with the people you serve.

For the sake of simplification, each page contains a healing tool, presented as a theme, the Verse of the Quran that refers to it, a brief reflection, and an activity explaining how it is applied.

This is not a therapy or self-help book. These are Tools to Consider. Some might be helpful, while others may not apply to you. Your story is unique, so please take care of your unique needs, be kind to your heart, and **console your soul.**

Multiple cohorts have contributed valuable insights to this initiative, and for that, I am forever grateful. This is still a work in progress. Please reach out with suggestions on how it can be improved at: **dromarareda@gmail.com**

Even though these tools are based on the Holy Quran, many of them are helpful for trauma survivors regardless of their faith background. We all are "children of God".

With gratitude and sincere appreciation, it is my absolute pleasure and honor to welcome you now to join me on a journey through…..*Healing Possibilities*.

1. Gratitude

Chapter 1, Verse 2 (All praise is for Allah, Lord of all worlds)

No one is more deserving of praise than Allah, and no amount of gratitude can truly match what He is worthy of.

While people often express gratitude through words, true thankfulness is reflected in our actions—through acts of appreciation.

Trauma can make it incredibly hard to feel grateful. When we are hurting, it can feel like there is nothing good left to hold onto. The mind can become so focused on pain and survival that blessings become hard to see. Yet, one of the most powerful tools in trauma healing is learning to notice—even in the smallest things—what we can still be grateful for.

Gratitude does not erase the pain, but rather gently reminds us that hardship is not our whole story.

Name three things or three people you are grateful for.

2. Service

Chapter 2, Verse 3 (And donate from what We have provided for them)

Allah calls upon us to give from what He has blessed us with—not only from our material wealth, but also from the many other gifts He has bestowed upon us. These include our time, knowledge, energy, skills, and compassion—resources that trauma can often make us forget we possess.

When we are in survival mode or carrying emotional wounds, it can feel like we have nothing left to offer. Trauma can blur our ability to recognize our own value. Yet, even the smallest act—a smile, a kind word, a listening ear—can be a form of charity and a reminder that we still carry light within us.

Being of service to others requires that we also tend to our own needs. As the saying goes, you cannot pour from an empty cup, when we care for ourselves—gently and intentionally—we restore the capacity to give to others from a place of authenticity, not depletion.

Did you help someone in need, within your capacity, today? What are the hidden gifts in that encounter—for them, and for you?

3. Intentionality

Chapter 2, Verse 9 (They seek to deceive Allah and the believers)

Human beings have been given free will and are accountable for their actions. With that freedom comes the ability to rise to the highest heights or to fall to the lowest depths.

Trauma can make us forget that we have agency. When we have been hurt, especially repeatedly or over time, we may begin to feel powerless like life is just happening to us, and we are merely surviving. This disconnection from our sense of choice is one of trauma's deepest wounds. Reclaiming our agency begins with intention. When we examine why we do what we do, we take a small but powerful step toward healing. Intention gives meaning to action, even in pain. It reminds us that we are not defined by what happened to us, but by how we choose to move forward.

What was your intention behind the deeds of today?

4. Grounding

Chapter 2, Verse 23 (And if you are in doubt)

Not associating partners with Allah goes beyond avoiding the worship of idols. It also means recognizing that false gods can be anything we place above Allah in our hearts, whether it is our family, wealth, ego, status, desires, or even our fears.

Trauma can quietly take up residence in the heart, filling it with anxiety, confusion, and a constant sense of threat. When we have been hurt or overwhelmed, our attention often shifts from Divine trust to survival mode. We may cling to control, people, or things in an attempt to feel safe. But healing begins when we return our hearts to Allah even in the middle of our pain....especially in the middle of our pain. Grounding is one way to support this return. It helps us reconnect to the current moment, quiet the noise of past wounds, and remember where true safety lies—not in control, but in surrender.

What is occupying and anchoring your heart today?

5. Appreciation

Chapter 2, Verse 25 (They will have pure spouses)

Allah wants us to enter Paradise not alone, but together with our loved ones. That is a goal worth striving for, one that gives meaning to our relationships and our efforts.

Trauma can make it difficult to express love in healthy ways. For some, it creates emotional distance—we shut down, go numb, or withdraw. For others, it stirs up anger or irritability, we lash out, and the easiest targets for these big, unresolved emotions are often those closest to us: our family. These patterns do not make us bad—they are often protective responses we learned to survive.

Islam calls us to rise above these cycles through awareness, compassion, and intentional action. Healing begins when we choose to act from our values rather than our wounds. Be available to your loved ones not just physically, but emotionally and spiritually. Even a few moments of genuine connection can repair ruptures and strengthen bonds.

Carve out intentional quality time today, and on a daily basis, to reconnect with those you love.

6. Be a Trustee

Chapter 2, Verse 30 (Remember when your Lord said to the angels, "I am going to place a successive ˹human˺ authority on earth")

To be a guardian of this earth is a sacred responsibility. It means remembering that one of the best ways to worship the Creator is serving His creation, with mercy, justice, and humility.

Trauma can distort how we see ourselves. It can cause us to question our worth, silence our voice, and disconnect from the purpose we were created for. When we carry the weight of unhealed pain, we may feel too broken or too unworthy to believe we could be entrusted with anything Divine. Yet, Allah has honored the believer with the role of His trustee on earth. To live with that awareness is to carry ourselves with humility, not arrogance, and with strength rooted in Divine connection. We must remind ourselves, and each other, that we are not defined by our stories, but by the One who entrusted us with this mission and who can heal our wounds. Every small act of care, kindness, or justice is a fulfillment of that trust.

What are three qualities of Allah's trustee? What do they carry in their heart, and how do they walk on earth?

7. Authenticity

Chapter 2, Verse 44 (Do you preach righteousness and fail to practice it yourselves?)

Islam teaches us to live with integrity—to practice what we invite others to do and to be the same person in private as we are in public. This consistency is not just about appearances; it is about sincerity and striving to align our actions with our values.

Trauma can create internal conflicts that make this difficult. When we have been hurt, we may act in ways that do not fully reflect our beliefs, not because we lack faith, but because we are operating from a place of pain, fear, or emotional exhaustion. Trauma can cloud our judgment, dull our sense of self, or cause us to react instead of respond. It is part of being human to fall short, sometimes.

Islam does not demand perfection; it invites self-awareness, humility, and a return to the path whenever we stray. The key is not to deny or hide our mistakes, but to acknowledge them, learn from them, and seek ways to repair what we can, with ourselves, with others, and with Allah.

Did your actions today align with your words and values? If not, how can you do better tomorrow?

8. Study History

Chapter 2, Verse 49 (´Remember` how We delivered you from the people of Pharaoh)

Allah calls us to reflect on the stories of past nations, not just to study history, but also to learn from it. Through these reflections, we are guided to avoid repeating the same mistakes and to recognize the patterns that lead to both rise and downfall.

When the Ummah is going through hardship, it can be hard to see clearly. Trauma, whether personal or collective, can cloud our thinking, distort our perspective, and lead us into hopelessness. We may become so overwhelmed by pain and grief that we lose sight of the bigger picture, feeling stuck in mourning rather than moving toward healing. The Quran reminds us: others before us have struggled too with injustice, loss, fear, and confusion. Through their stories, we are shown that no matter how chaotic or broken things may seem, Allah is always in control. He restores order, brings justice, and lifts people out of despair, often in ways they never expected.

What can you learn from the fate of one of the past nations mentioned in the Quran? How does their story speak to your personal or collective struggle today?

9. Take Nothing for Granted

Chapter 2, Verse 61 (Do you exchange what is better for what is worse?)

Many times, we take Allah's blessings for granted or even reject them, especially when we trade something of high spiritual value for a fleeting worldly gain. We might overlook what truly matters in favor of what simply feels easier, more familiar, or immediately rewarding.

Man loves instant gratification. Trauma can blur our vision and block our ability to recognize the blessings that remain. It often narrows our focus to what was lost, broken, or painful; making it difficult to see the goodness that trauma did not take away. We may forget to notice the small mercies, the quiet strengths, or the moments of beauty and tenderness still present in our lives. When we begin to work through our trauma, we can start to remove the "dark glasses" of despair. Slowly, we learn to shift from only seeing what is missing to also noticing what has endured and what is still whole within and around us.

What are three blessings in your life that you tend to overlook or take for granted?

10. Soften Your Heart

Chapter 2, Verse 74 (Even then your hearts became hardened like a rock or even harder)

Allah describes some hearts as being "harder than rocks", but this is not a death sentence. Even the hardest heart can soften with Allah's mercy. The beloved Prophet was known for his gentle heart, and he showed us many ways to soften ours through caring for the orphans, serving those in need, and living with compassion and grace.

Trauma can deeply affect the state of the heart. A heart full of pain may harden, not out of harshness, but as a defense mechanism. After experiencing betrayal, abuse, or emotional neglect, many people find it difficult to trust, to open up, or to feel safe in vulnerability. That guardedness is a form of self-protection, especially when the world has felt unsafe or unkind. Healing often begins when we shift our focus in healthy and intentional ways. Looking after others can be a powerful way to reconnect with our own humanity. Acts of service do not just benefit those we help; they also help us rebuild trust in ourselves and in the goodness of people. Giving from a place of sincerity creates small bridges where walls once stood.

How can you begin, or continue, to care for those in need around you, especially your family and relatives? What small acts of kindness, support, or presence can you offer God's creation today?

10

11. Mend People's Hearts

Chapter 2, Verse 83 (Speak kindly to people)

Allah commands us to speak only words of grace, and Islam teaches that we should either say something kind—or remain silent. This is not just about politeness; it is about cultivating a heart that uplifts rather than harms.

Trauma can narrow our window of tolerance. When we are overwhelmed, anxious, or dysregulated, our ability to be patient, compassionate, or thoughtful in our speech often diminishes. We may react harshly, shut down emotionally, or say things we later regret, not because we lack good character, but because our nervous system is on the defense. Part of healing is learning to pause before we react. It means slowing down, paying attention to our triggers, and building emotional awareness. Watching our words starts with watching what is happening inside of us. And to truly grow, we must be open to feedback, recognizing that the way we come across may not always match our intentions.

How can you be more mindful of your words today? In what situations might silence be more healing than speaking? And how can you make room for grace, even when you are struggling to show up with kindness?

12. Rethink Death

Chapter 2, Verse 96 (You will surely find them clinging to life)

Most people love life and fear or dislike death. Islam teaches us that death is not the end; it is simply one stop on the journey toward our final destination. It is a transition, not a disappearance.

When we lose someone we love, grief can feel overwhelming. But the weight of that grief may ease when we remember that their departure is not permanent. For the believer, separation in this life is followed by the promise of eternal reunion in Paradise, where pain and parting no longer exist. Still, fearing or hating death is normal, especially for those who have lived through trauma. Painful losses, sudden tragedies, or near-death experiences can leave behind emotional scars that make the idea of death terrifying. Trauma can also shake our sense of safety and control, which can make death feel like an unbearable unknown. It is important to explore these fears with compassion, not shaming. Understanding why we fear death can be the first step in healing our relationship with it and deepening our trust in Allah's mercy and Divine plan.

Do you fear or hate death? What experiences or beliefs might be contributing to that inner experience?

13. Allah is in Control

Chapter 2, Verse 107 (Do you not know that the kingdom of the heavens and the earth belongs ˹only˺ to Allah)

Trauma can leave people feeling profoundly alone and unsupported. It can create the painful illusion that no one understands, no one cares, and that even Allah is distant. These feelings are common and they are part of the normal response to trauma.

This Verse reminds us of an unshakable truth: Allah does whatever He wills in His dominion. While that might sound overwhelming at first, it is also a deep source of comfort, because the One who is in control is also the Most Merciful and the Most Gentle. Realizing that Allah Himself is our ultimate source of support can bring reassurance, especially when human support is lacking or has failed us. His decree is not random. It is purposeful, even when painful. And with every hardship He decrees, He also promises ease, guidance, and healing.

When you feel alone in the aftermath of trauma, try to ask yourself: Can I believe, even just a little, that Allah has chosen this test for me, and that He will help me through it?

14. Be a Safety Source

Chapter 2, Verse 114 (Who does more wrong than those who prevent Allah's Name from being mentioned in His places of worship and strive to destroy them?)

We should never be the reason anyone feels unsafe, especially in the House of Allah. The masjid belongs to Allah alone. It is meant to be a sanctuary, a place of peace and mercy, open to all who seek Him. No one has the right to treat others with harshness, judgment, or exclusion, whether inside or outside a place of worship. Yet, sadly, many worshippers, especially youth, women, reverts, and those struggling with their faith, report feeling unwelcome or even alienated in the very space meant to draw them closer to Allah.

For individuals carrying the weight of trauma, rejection in spiritual spaces can be especially devastating, reinforcing feelings of shame, isolation, or spiritual unworthiness. It can turn a house of healing into another place of harm.

Did you help someone feel safe, seen, or welcomed today? How can you contribute to making spaces you are part of more inclusive, especially for those who are hurting or hesitant to come close?

15. Submit

Chapter 2, Verse 131 (When his Lord ordered him, "Submit to My Will," he responded, "I submit to the Lord of all worlds")

Prophet Abraham earned the title of the intimate friend of Allah because of his unwavering willingness to submit to his Lord's commands without hesitation, even when the tests were unimaginably difficult.

True submission requires letting go of control and that can be incredibly hard for those who have experienced trauma. For many trauma survivors, the last time they let their guard down, they were hurt, betrayed, or left unprotected. As a result, control can become a survival strategy, a way to feel safe in a world that once felt dangerous or unpredictable. But surrendering to Allah is not the same as surrendering to harm. It is not about being passive, it is about trusting that the One who decrees your tests also equips you with the strength, wisdom, and insight to transform and grow through them.

What represents the foundation of your home? What does trauma exposure look like for you? How do you protect and nurture your family after going through adversity? And how do you submit to the will of Allah when tested with something deeply painful?

16. Bear Witness

Chapter 2, Verse 140 (Who does more wrong than those who hide the testimony they received from Allah?)

Truth-telling is not just a moral virtue in Islam, it is a sacred responsibility.

One of the most painful and disempowering tests a person can endure is witnessing evil, oppression, or violence and feeling unable to stop it. This helplessness can be emotionally paralyzing. For trauma survivors, this feeling is especially familiar: watching harm unfold and being unable to intervene, sometimes even losing their voice in the process. One example of this is the current situation in Palestine and other parts of the Muslim Ummah, where we are witnessing horrific atrocities—children and civilians being displaced, starved, bombed, and subjected to ethnic cleansing. The weight of witnessing this brutality can trigger profound sorrow, rage, numbness, or despair. But Islam reminds us that the believer is never truly powerless.

How can you care for the oppressed, while also tending to your own well-being? How can you speak your truth and use your voice to speak up for those who have been silenced?

17. Faith in Action

Chapter 2, Verse 143 (Allah would never discount your ʿprevious acts ofʾ faith)

Allah teaches us not to belittle "small" bad deeds because they can gradually build up and lead to major sins. At the same time, we are reminded not to underestimate the power of "small" good deeds because even the tiniest act of kindness or sincerity could be our ticket to Paradise. Nothing is lost with Allah.

Sin can weigh heavily on the soul, creating feelings of shame, guilt, and spiritual defeat. For those carrying trauma, these feelings may be amplified, as past wounds can distort how we see ourselves, making us feel unworthy of forgiveness or redemption. But repentance is a path back to restoring dignity, and engaging in acts of grace toward ourselves and others can uplift us spiritually and emotionally. Every small effort to tend to our inner wounds, to speak gently to ourselves, or to show mercy, is a step forward on our healing journey.

Draw a plane. One wing represents fear of disappointing Allah. The other represents love for His mercy. Fuel the plane with the hope that no matter how heavy your past or how deep your pain, Allah can carry you forward.

18. Patience

Chapter 2, Verse 155 (Give good news to those who patiently endure)

Patience holds a special and elevated place in Islam. It is one of the few acts that Allah promises to reward without measure on the Day of Judgment. It is not passive endurance, it is an active, courageous response rooted in faith. Patience does not mean staying silent in toxic environments, enduring abuse, or remaining stuck in oppressive systems. True patience is not about tolerating harm. It is taking the necessary steps to protect yourself, seek justice, or change your circumstances and then trusting Allah with the outcome.

For survivors of trauma, patience often looks different. It may look like choosing not to retaliate, speaking up when it is hard, walking away from harmful people, or simply getting through the day without giving up. That, too, is patience. And in Allah's eyes, it carries immense weight.

Name three things that people have done to hurt you. How did you face that pain with patience, boundaries, or grace?

19. Defeat Evil Thoughts

Chapter 2, Verse 168 (And do not follow Satan's footsteps)

Allah does not only warn us against following the devil's plans, He also cautions us not to follow even his whispers and footsteps. This includes entertaining negative, harmful, or deceptive thoughts. Why? Because thoughts can lead to feelings, feelings can shape actions, and actions can form habits that can eventually become our character and lifestyle.

For trauma survivors, this process can be especially challenging. Trauma often leaves the mind flooded with intrusive or automatic negative thoughts about the world, about others, and especially about the self. These thoughts can be intense, persistent, and rooted in past pain rather than present truth. The devil preys on these vulnerabilities, feeding hopelessness, self-blame, fear, and despair. But we are not powerless. One way to resist these whispers is to build a healing structure into your day through a balanced routine, acts of service, and purposeful living. Another essential tool is choosing the right companions.

How are you currently coping with automatic negative thoughts?

20. Never Hide the Truth

Chapter 2, Verse 174 (Indeed, those who hide Allah's revelations)

Islam is a faith deeply rooted in truth and justice. The Quran consistently emphasizes justice as a core value, one that applies not only to societal systems, but also to our relationships, conversations, and the way we treat one another's experiences and our own.

Denying someone's truth or dismissing their lived experience can be deeply harmful. For individuals who have gone through trauma, invalidation can feel like a second wound, one that often cuts even deeper than the original stab, adding insult to injury. When someone shares their story and is met with disbelief, minimization, or silencing, it reinforces the message that their voice does not matter.

Islam teaches us to bear witness with honesty and compassion. Recognizing someone's pain does not mean you agree with every detail, it means you are present, listening, and offering dignity to their truth.

When someone opens their heart and shares their story with you: Do you truly take the time to listen? Or do you feel the urge to fix, advise, problem-solve, or insert your own experience into their moment?

21. Grace

Chapter 2, Verse 177 (Who give charity out of their cherished wealth to relatives, orphans, the poor, ˹needy˼ travelers, beggars, and for freeing captives)

Islam is not only about the physical rituals of worship or matters of creed. Those are undeniably foundational, but at its heart, Islam calls us to care for those in need and to spend from what we love most. This includes our time, energy, and resources.

Man-made traumas, such as the aftermath of armed conflicts, forced displacement, and social injustice, deeply wound individuals and communities. Yet, these painful experiences also open unique opportunities for healing through acts of compassion like volunteerism, community service, and mutual support. Engaging in these graceful activities not only aids others but also nurtures our own spiritual and emotional growth.

Draw a pyramid with three levels: At the bottom, Islam (submission). In the middle, Iman (faith). At the top, Ihsan (excellence and grace). What steps can you take to reach the level of Ihsan in your daily life?

22. Certainty

Chapter 2, Verse 186 (When My servants ask you ˹O Prophet˺ about Me: I am truly near. I respond to one's prayer when they call upon Me)

Allah intends ease for us, not hardship. He hears our supplications and responds, sometimes immediately, and other times after a delay that is best for our growth and healing. Trusting that Allah's plan is the best plan, even when we cannot see the full picture, is a profound act of faith.

For trauma survivors, who often live with uncertainty, pain, and feelings of loss of control, holding on to this certainty can be a powerful anchor. It helps put struggles into perspective and offers hope that healing and relief will come in due time.

After each prayer, sit quietly with the deep certainty of Allah's promise to answer your prayers. Let this moment be one of surrender, hope, and inner peace even if the answer has not yet arrived.

23. Sacred Contract

Chapter 2, Verse 187 (Your spouses are a garment for you as you are for them)

A husband and wife are like garments for one another. Just as a garment covers, comforts, protects, and beautifies, spouses are meant to provide shelter, warmth, security, and grace to each other. Islam teaches us to treat our spouses with tender loving care, kindness, and patience.

Trauma has the power to shape or shake us, not only as individuals but also within our families, communities, and societies. When spouses nurture a sacred, supportive relationship, it can become a strong and healing foundation, especially for children affected by trauma. A healthy marital bond can serve as a grounding refuge, offering safety and stability in the midst of life's storms.

What are three different ways the Quran describes the marriage relationship? How can you embody and put these beautiful descriptions into action in your own family? And even if you are not married yet, can building a safe household be one of your future goals?

24. Honor Allah's Boundaries

Chapter 2, Verse 193 (Let there be no hostility except against the aggressors)

Islam permits self-defense, such as fighting against militants, but strictly prohibits transgression, including harming innocent civilians.

Unfortunately, some people use their hands and tongues not as tools for healing, but as weapons for wounding. When we are deeply hurt, it can feel natural to want revenge or to go to extremes. But no matter how wounded we are, we must never exceed Allah's limits in the pursuit of justice. True justice in Islam is balanced by mercy, restraint, and respect for the dignity of all human beings.

The 5H exercise: What is your duty towards your: Head, Heart, Hand, Home, and towards Humanity?

25. Avoid Judging Others

Chapter 2, Verse 204 (There are some ˹hypocrites˺ who impress you with their views regarding worldly affairs)

We may find ourselves impressed by someone because of the way they look, speak, or carry themselves in public. But what we see on the outside does not always reflect the truth. Behind closed doors, a person might engage in harmful behaviors like acts of injustice, deceit, or corruption that are hidden from public view but visible to Allah. At the same time, someone who appears insignificant in the eyes of people may be among the most beloved to Allah.

Trauma can distort a person's behavior, emotional expression, or ability to connect. Many trauma survivors are misunderstood, dismissed, or judged harshly because of how they show up in the world. But Islam teaches us to look deeper, with empathy instead of judgment. Believing in someone's ability to heal, change, and grow, especially when they do not yet believe it themselves, can be a powerful part of their recovery. Your trust in them may become a mirror that helps them see their beauty.

Think of three companions of the Prophet who were invisible to the people, but seen by Allah and His Messenger.

26. Never Give Up

Chapter 2, Verse 214 (Even the Messenger and the believers with him cried out, "When will Allah's help come?")

It is part of human nature to come close to despair at times, especially when pain feels unrelenting and the future seems uncertain. But in the moments when things are at their worst, relief from Allah is often closest. Allah promises that with hardship comes ease. Not after it, but with it. Sometimes, what appears to be breaking us is actually preparing us for healing, growth, and transformation.

For survivors of trauma, this reminder is especially important. Trauma can conceal hope and make the heart feel abandoned. Remembering that even the most beloved of creation suffered and still held onto Allah's mercy can motivate us to heal.

Write down three difficulties you are currently facing, and then beneath each one, write down the options available to you. Always remember: Giving up on Allah's mercy is never an option.

27. A Silver Lining

Chapter 2, Verse 216 (Perhaps you dislike something which is good for you)

Our knowledge is limited. What we see is only a fragment of the full picture. Sometimes, we dislike something that is actually good for us, and other times we are drawn to something that may ultimately harm us. This is why trusting in Allah's Divine wisdom is so essential, because He sees what we cannot.

Trauma can cloud our vision, making the world seem dark, heavy, and hopeless. The pain of injustice, war, loss, or betrayal can feel all-encompassing like a thick cloud that blocks out the light. Yet, even within the darkest of storms, Allah's mercy continues to flow. There is always something, however small, that carries goodness, growth, or awakening. Sometimes, what looks like devastation may carry the seeds of transformation, and what feels like a breaking point might actually be a turning point.

Is there a positive side to the difficulties the Ummah is facing right now? What is one possible blessing wrapped inside this severe hardship?

28. Know Your Worth

Chapter 2, Verse 221 (They invite ˹you˺ to the Fire while Allah invites ˹you˺ to Paradise and forgiveness)

Islam teaches us not to be attracted only to outward appearances. True beauty lies in the heart, the soul, and the character of a person. It is not in the perfection of features, but in the sincerity of spirit.

Trauma has the power to distort how we see ourselves. It can convince survivors that they are unworthy, broken, or unlovable. Many internalize messages of shame and invisibility, believing that their pain has somehow made them less beautiful or less whole. Part of the healing journey is reclaiming our narrative, realizing that we can gather the scattered pieces of our story, the ones trauma tried to shatter, and use them to rebuild a version of ourselves that is wiser, stronger, and more compassionate. Healing does not mean returning to who you were before trauma. It means becoming someone even more grounded and real because of what you have been through.

Draw a broken heart. Inside each fragment, write a word or phrase that represents part of your story, whether it is loss, growth, hope, or others. Then, reflect on the quote by Rumi: "You have to keep breaking your heart until it opens".

29. Allah is Watching

Chapter 2, Verse 235 (Know that Allah is aware of what is in your hearts, so beware of Him)

Allah knows what is hidden in the hearts of His creation. His knowledge encompasses the unseen, the unspoken, and even the emotions we struggle to understand. Nothing escapes His awareness, not a silent tear, not a broken hope, and not a single beat of the wounded heart.

For trauma survivors, this truth holds deep significance. When someone has been silenced, whether by fear, shame, disbelief, or the cruelty of others, they may begin to feel voiceless, invisible, or forgotten. The inability to share one's story can feel like an added trauma. But knowing that Allah sees and hears us even when the world does not, offers a source of relief and validation that no human being can replicate. Even when no one else knows what you have endured, Allah knows. Even when no one else believes you, Allah believes in you. Even when you cannot say it, Allah knows it.

Allah sees your heart. What does it carry? Why would Allah, who sees all injustice and oppression, allow it to happen?

30. Be Among the Few

Chapter 2, Verse 243 (Surely Allah is ever Bountiful to humanity, but most people are ungrateful)

Allah gives out of His infinite mercy, not because we are always deserving or grateful. Despite the constant blessings we receive, most of His servants remain heedless or ungrateful, yet He continues to provide, forgive, and guide. A true believer strives to be among the few who show sincere appreciation, not just through words, but also through actions that align with Allah's instructions and values.

But let us be honest: when our wounds are still bleeding and our hearts are aching, it can feel incredibly difficult to offer thanks. Gratitude may seem far away when life is heavy, when trauma silences the soul, or when we are just trying to survive. Yet, there are those rare individuals, "the chosen few", who are able to see the gift within the test. They find light in the darkness, strength in surrender, and growth in grief. This level of spiritual maturity does not mean ignoring the pain, it means trusting that Allah is present within it.

Search the Quran for three Verses where Allah mentions that most of His creation follow their desires, while only a few are grateful.

31. Lead, Do Not Follow

Chapter 2, Verse 249 (How many times has a small force vanquished a mighty army by the Will of Allah)

Some people are easily impressed by individuals or causes simply because they are popular or trending. But Islam teaches us that truth is not measured by popularity, and that believers are not meant to blindly follow trends, they are meant to lead by example. Our legacy as Muslims is not to seek fame or follow the crowd, but to make the world a better place. True belief can turn one person into a nation, even if they are walking the path toward Allah alone. Many Prophets were sent to communities that rejected them. Some had very few, or no, followers. But that never diminished their value, their impact, or their closeness to Allah.

In today's world, marked by mass suffering, injustice, and forgotten victims, this lesson is especially important. The graves of many are nameless. The trauma of war, displacement, and systemic violence has silenced countless stories. Yet Allah knows every name, every wound, and every story.

Name three things that currently impress you. Do they align with Islamic values?

32. Quran's Greatest Verse

Chapter 2, Verse 255 (Allah! There is no god ˈworthy of worshipˈ except Him, the Ever-Living, All-Sustaining)

This Verse is one of Allah's greatest gifts to the Ummah. The beloved Prophet would recite it multiple times each day, recognizing its immense power. Many Verses in the Quran serve not only as spiritual guidance but also as part of a trauma-healing toolkit, especially this one.

When the soul feels broken, and when the heart carries heavy wounds, the words of Allah can become a source of grounding, comfort, and strength. For those navigating grief, fear, anxiety, or the aftermath of deep pain, reflecting on this Verse can help bring clarity and soothe the turmoil within. It reminds us that we are never alone, that Allah is always near, and that His mercy is greater than any trial we face.

Memorize this Verse. Recite it regularly, especially in moments of distress, uncertainty, or emotional heaviness. And deeply reflect on its meanings.

33. Give Your Best

Chapter 2, Verse 267 (Donate from the best of what you have earned)

A true believer gives only from what is ḥalal and pure, because Allah does not accept anything except what is wholesome and sincere. Intent matters. Purity of intention, source, and purpose elevates the act of giving in the eyes of Allah. One of the most profound lessons we learn from the poor is their generosity. Those who have the least are often those who give the most, with sincerity, humility, and open hearts. People who visit the forgotten, like those in prisons, refugee camps, shelters, or care homes, often come away spiritually enriched, deeply moved by how people with almost nothing still find ways to give, share, and uplift others.

Trauma survivors, especially those in need, often live with layers of invisible grief, but within them also lies profound strength, compassion, and faith. While giving, they share, whether a smile, a prayer, or a piece of bread, reminders that giving is not about how much we have, but how much we care.

What can you give right now to help improve the situation of the Ummah? Even if going through your own healing journey, can you still be a source of healing for others?

33

34. Search for the Invisible

Chapter 2, Verse 273 (Those unfamiliar with their situation will think they are not in need)

Allah commands us to care for those who are often invisible, the ones who come and go without being noticed, who silently struggle, and who would rather go to bed hungry than ask for help. These are the people who, in their humility and dignity, conceal their pain from the world, but never from Allah.

 Trauma can cause people to withdraw, to shrink into isolation, avoid connection, and detach from the very support systems that could help them heal. As a community, we are responsible for each other. It is not enough to wait for someone to reach out, we must be proactive in our compassion and attention, especially toward those who are most likely to be overlooked.

Have you searched for, and tended to, the needs of someone "invisible" today? Empower them with discretion and grace.

35. Look from a Different Angle

Chapter 2, Verse 286 (Allah does not require of any soul more than what it can afford)

Allah promises that He does not test any soul beyond what it can bear. Yet, trauma has the power to cloud our thinking, distort our judgment, and narrow our vision.

When weighed down by pain, it can feel as if the burden is unbearable and that no options remain. This is a natural response to overwhelming hardship; it is the mind's way of protecting itself by focusing on the immediate context. But it can also trap us in despair, preventing us from seeing the full picture and the many healing possibilities.

When you feel overwhelmed, how can you consciously try to step back and view the issue from a different perspective? What might Allah be teaching you through this trial?

36. Aim High

Chapter 3, Verse 15 (Say, ˹O Prophet,˺ "Shall I inform you of what is better than ˹all of˺ this?")

Many people are naturally attracted and attached to the pleasures of this life. While Islam does not forbid enjoying permissible worldly blessings, it teaches us to channel both our energy and focus toward the ultimate goal: attaining Paradise. Islam is about maintaining focus and keeping our eyes fixed on the true, eternal reward—the "trophy" that surpasses all temporary gains.

Trauma can often cloud this vision. It can trap us in the pain, where our attention is consumed by immediate needs, making it difficult to see beyond the hardship. This narrowed focus can leave us feeling stuck, overwhelmed, and disconnected from our greater purpose and potential.

Draw a high bar representing your goals. Write down some realistic, manageable goals. And celebrate "small" victories.

37. Participate

Chapter 3, Verse 17 ('It is they' who are patient, sincere, obedient, and charitable, and who pray for forgiveness before dawn)

Allah has prepared Paradise for those who engage in all kinds of good deeds, seeking only the pleasure of their Lord.

One powerful tool for healing the wounds of trauma is to participate in communal activities and acts of service. For example, a Palestinian man who referred to his granddaughter, who was killed in Gaza, as "the soul of my soul", found a path to healing by becoming a "one-man relief agency," dedicating himself to helping others in need. Also, the beloved Prophet encouraged his companions to engage in serving their community as a means of coping with adversity. Through service, we can transform our pain into purpose.

Envision the eight doors of Paradise, each representing different paths of righteous deeds and mercy. How do you plan to strive to enter through each of these doors?

38. Allah's Open Door

Chapter 3, Verse 28 (Allah warns you about Himself)

Allah wants His creation to be mindful of Him, for to Him they will all return. Believers must continuously return to Allah's door whenever they err or fall short, and non-believers are always invited to knock on the door of their Master. We are encouraged to think only good of Him, no matter how greatly we may have messed up.

Trauma can cause some people to feel distant from their faith, especially if they turn to unhealthy coping mechanisms to numb their pain. This distance can feel isolating, making it seem as if the door to Allah's mercy is closed. But the truth is, no matter how far we stray, Allah's door of redemption remains wide open, always.

Envision a door that is always open, even when all other doors in your life feel closed or locked tight. How does it feel to know that Allah's mercy is accessible, no matter what you have been through?

39. Love is Action

Chapter 3, Verse 31 (Say, ˹O Prophet,˺ "If you ˹sincerely˺ love Allah, then follow me; Allah will love you")

Love is not merely a claim or empty words; true love is shown through actions. You cannot truly claim to love your Lord while continuing to disobey Him. The path to loving Allah is to follow the example and teachings of His beloved Prophet PBUH.

Unfortunately, some Muslims experience religious trauma, where they associate their wounds and pain with Islam itself. This is heartbreaking. Islam is perfect, but Muslims are human and therefore imperfect. At times, certain community or faith leaders misuse the name of the religion or take text out of context to serve their own personal agendas, causing harm and confusion to many. This misuse can leave deep scars, making it difficult for trauma survivors to feel safe within their faith. But our role-model if Muhammad, and the beloved Prophet never hurt anyone. He taught us that a true Muslim is someone whose hand and tongue bring safety and comfort to others, not injuries.

What are three ways you express your love towards Allah and the beloved Prophet? How can your actions, especially while coping with trauma, reflect this love?

40. Be a Role-Model

Chapter 3, Verse 38 (My Lord! Grant me—by your grace—righteous offspring)

Children learn most powerfully by example. When parents shut down emotionally or lash out instead of processing their feelings in healthy ways, children may internalize the message that emotions are dangerous, to be feared, avoided, or dismissed. As a result, these children might suffer in silence, cry themselves to sleep, or, even worse, turn to self-harm or unhealthy coping mechanisms or the wrong crowd to soothe their pain. Parents have a profound responsibility and opportunity to model healthy, safe ways to process difficult emotions and experiences. By showing vulnerability and constructive emotional expression, parents teach their children that even big feelings are natural and manageable.

How do you care for your children after trauma?

41. Lean on Allah

Chapter 3, Verse 55 (Then to Me you will ˹all˺ return, and I will settle all your disputes)

People may plot against you or scheme to harm you, but rest assured that Allah also has His plans. He defends the believers, and His plan is always the most perfect plan.

Holding this belief deep in your heart can bring comfort and strength, especially when you are trying to make sense of the painful or confusing events you have experienced. Meaning-making is a vital part of how humans process, navigate, and ultimately heal from trauma. It helps us find purpose or lessons even in hardship.

The next time you feel scared or overwhelmed, can you pause and recognize that you are leaning on Allah for support and protection?

42. Unmask

Chapter 3, Verse 66 (Allah knows and you do not know)

Many of us wear different masks in different situations, often for various reasons.

Trauma can cause people to behave differently in front of others, sometimes hiding their true feelings or struggles. One painful byproduct of trauma is secrecy. Survivors often "keep the secret" out of fear of "burdening" others or being judged.

Islam encourages us to live authentically and to heal through human and Divine connection. It calls us to gently open up to our loved ones and to the support systems Allah has created for our healing and well-being. Breaking the silence can be the first step toward relief and genuine recovery from the weight of trauma. Breaking the silence can break the cycle.

Are you wearing a mask? What purpose does it serve? What do you need to take it off?

43. Embody the Divine Names

Chapter 3, Verse 79 (Be devoted to the worship of your Lord ˹alone˺)

The entire universe submits humbly to the will of its Lord, yet humans often walk arrogantly, forgetting where they came from.

The names of Allah serve as a profound source of reflection, spiritual connection, and healing. For trauma survivors, embodying the beautiful attributes of Allah can help rebuild compassion — both for ourselves and for others — even when our hearts feel broken or burdened. By embracing these Divine qualities, we can expand our capacity to heal and to relate with kindness, patience, and mercy.

Write down the 99 Names of Allah. Choose one attribute each week to embody, allowing it to guide your healing journey.

44. Be a Light Source

Chapter 3, Verse 92 (You will never achieve righteousness until you donate some of what you cherish)

You will achieve the highest level of faith only when you spend from what you love most, not just your money, but also sharing your light with others so they, too, can discover or rediscover their light.

Trauma has the power to dim our inner light, leaving us feeling lost, disconnected, and depleted. Yet, our support systems like our family, friends, community, and faith, can guide us back to the source of light within ourselves that needs to be found, protected, and nurtured.

What are three blessings you have been given that you can share with others?

45. Try Your Best

Chapter 3, Verse 104 (Let there be a group among you)

Allah advises us to strive to die in a state of devotion to Him, to hold tightly to His rope, to avoid division, to appreciate His countless blessings, and to enjoin good while forbidding evil. By embodying these principles, we qualify to be "the best nation".

Looking at the current struggles and suffering faced by the Ummah, it is natural to question whether we are truly deserving of Allah's victory. Trauma and hardship can shake, weaken, and disconnect us from our faith. Yet, we must remember that life can change in the blink of an eye, by Allah's will, transforming defeat into victory and turning despair into hope.

What are three characteristics of the best nation that you can embody during difficult times?

46. Be Fair

Chapter 3, Verse 113 (Yet they are not all alike)

During these divisive times, it is especially important that we do not transgress or respond to hate with more hatred.

When we are victims of injustice or aggression, it can be easy to develop resentment or distrust toward people from other backgrounds. Islam reminds us that every culture and religion has both good and bad within it. We must remain vigilant, but also open-hearted, without alienating potential allies who could support our healing and unity. Trauma can narrow our vision, making us see only walls where there might be bridges for shared humanity, understanding, and connection.

How do you perceive and relate to people from backgrounds different from your own, especially in light of your experiences with trauma?

47. Please Allah

Chapter 3, Verse 119 (May you˺ die of your rage!)

Many of us avoid confrontation and try to please everyone, even those who have hurt us deeply.

Trauma can make it hard to set boundaries, as we may fear rejection or conflict. It is important to remember that some people will dislike or even hate you no matter what you do, and sometimes, for no reason at all. You will never be able to please all of creation. Instead, focus on pleasing Allah, whose acceptance and mercy bring true peace and healing.

Is it truly possible to please the creation? How can you redirect your efforts toward pleasing the Creator instead?

48. A Clear Roadmap

Chapter 3, Verse 126 (Allah ordained this ˹reinforcement˺ as good news for you and reassurance for your hearts)

The ultimate goal for Muslims is to attain Allah's pleasure. The way to achieve this is through sincerity and steadfast adherence to the teachings of the Prophet.

Difficulties and adversity, especially traumatic experiences, can cause some to feel distant from their faith, while for others these challenges can deepen their connection and grounding in Islam. Trauma may shake our beliefs or make us question our purpose, but it can also become our turning point toward greater sincerity and devotion.

Draw a straight path illuminated by the light of sincere faith and the guidance of the Prophetic traditions. How are you following this Divine roadmap through your exhausting traumatic journey?

49. Compete for Paradise

Chapter 3, Verse 133 (And hasten towards forgiveness from your Lord and a Paradise as vast as the heavens and the earth, prepared for those mindful of Allah)

Allah gives us the glad tidings that He can forgive our bad deeds if we sincerely regret them and follow them with good deeds. It is the sincerity of our remorse that truly matters. Allah's door of mercy is always open as long as we keep knocking on it and turning to Him with humility. This beautiful Verse also reminds us that holding back anger and pardoning others can be a means to attain Paradise.

It is important to emphasize here that Islam does not condone being a silent victim. Trauma can deeply affect our emotions, and expressing pain, anger, or hurt is both natural and necessary for healing, provided it is done safely and constructively. We are not required to forgive others before we are ready or able to do so. Forgiveness is a choice, not an obligation.

How do you feel when you make a mistake? How is your attitude helping you on your path towards Paradise?

49

50. Martyrdom

Chapter 3, Verse 145 (No soul can ever die without Allah's Will at the destined time)

Trials and tribulations serve to distinguish true believers from hypocrites.

The greatest disaster for this Ummah was the passing of our beloved Prophet, many hearts were shaken that day, yet that never turned the true companions away from the Quran and Sunnah.

Remaining steadfast in both heart and action during times of uncertainty is a powerful sign of true faith. Trauma can shake our foundations, making it difficult to hold on, but it can also be a catalyst to deepen our reliance on Allah and strengthen our resolve.

What are three things you are doing to prepare yourself for meeting Allah?

51. Use Time Wisely

Chapter 3, Verse 152 (Some of you were after worldly gain while others desired a heavenly reward)

Allah warns us that if we obey our desires, we will go astray and be among the losers.

During difficult times, especially when we witness the Ummah weak and defeated, it is normal to question our faith and wrestle with deep existential doubts. Trauma and hardship often intensify negative feelings, making belief seem challenging or distant. Yet, no matter how tempting disbelief or despair may appear, true belief remains the source of hope, strength, and guidance. It anchors us amidst chaos and helps us rebuild from our brokenness.

What are three things that keep you occupied and focused on your faith and purpose during trying times?

52. The Wisdom Behind Testing

Chapter 3, Verse 154 (Through this, Allah tests what is within you and purifies what is in your hearts)

It is easy for a believer to follow the teachings of Islam during times of comfort and ease. However, true faith is tested through trials and hardships. These challenges expose what the heart truly contains and whether it remains steadfast, patient, and sincere, or falters under pressure.

For trauma survivors, these moments can be especially difficult, as pain and suffering may cloud one's connection to faith. Yet, it is precisely through patience and trust in Allah during these times that the heart grows stronger and healing begins.

How are you living the message of Islam, especially when that is not easy to do?

53. Be Gentle

Chapter 3, Verse 159 (It is out of Allah's mercy that you ⌐O Prophet⌐ have been lenient with them)

Allah praised the beloved Prophet's gentle demeanor and kind character. It is no wonder that people were drawn to his sweet and compassionate nature. Had he been harsh or hardhearted, many would have turned away and rejected the message he came to deliver.

Remaining consistently graceful and patient amid hardships is incredibly challenging, especially for those carrying wounds from trauma. Yet, the beloved Prophet, who faced the greatest tests and trials, maintained unwavering grace and mercy throughout his blessed life, regardless of the external circumstances. His example shows us that even in the darkest of times, kindness is still possible.

How do people perceive you? Are there any rough edges in your character that you can refine by following the beautiful example of the Prophet?

54. The Ultimate Safety

Chapter 3, Verse 173 (Allah ʿaloneˈ is sufficient ʿas an aidˈ for us and ʿHeˈ is the best Protector)

Those who lean on Allah find deep comfort and strength, even if the entire world conspires against them.

This supplication is one of the powerful prayers that sustained many Prophets and their followers during the most challenging and painful times.

For trauma survivors, when fear and uncertainty overwhelm the heart and mind, turning to Allah can be a refuge that restores a sense of safety.

When you feel scared or overwhelmed, how can you regain a sense of safety by strengthening your connection with Allah?

55. An Open Invitation

Chapter 3, Verse 178 (Disbelievers should not think that living longer is good for them. They are only given more time to increase in sin)

Islam is not a harsh religion. In fact, it is quite the opposite. Yet, those who intentionally hurt others will be given many chances to repent and change their ways. If they decide to ignore Allah's invitation to receive mercy, they will have nothing but regret the day they meet their Lord. Islam extends an open invitation to everyone to search for, and find, Allah.

Reflect on the Prophetic saying that "the best among the people is the one who is blessed with a long life that he spends in doing good"

56. Grief in Islam

Chapter 3, Verse 185 (Every soul will taste death)

Death is the only certainty in life. Everybody dies. What truly matters is not when we die, but how we meet our Lord.

Traumatic loss, especially sudden or violent death, can leave deep wounds that are hard to heal. Ambiguous loss, such as when a loved one is missing or emotionally unavailable, can cause prolonged suffering and confusion. That is why Islam permits grieving, recognizing it as a natural and necessary process. Grief is the price we pay for love. The only way to begin healing from grief is to allow ourselves to grieve. Death is the end of life, but not the end of a relationship. We should remember the deceased without the added weight of guilt, and also hold on to the good memories. One way to grieve a loved one is by repairing relationships with their relatives. Practicing self-care is another way to honor the dead, as it is what they would have wanted for us.

Can you set aside time, at least once a month, to visit your local cemetery? If you had only 24 hours left to live, what would you change about your life?

57. Home is Paradise

Chapter 3, Verse 195 (Those who migrated or were expelled from their homes, and were persecuted for My sake and fought and were martyred—I will certainly forgive their sins and admit them into Gardens under which rivers flow)

Allah rewards those who are forcibly displaced and compelled to flee their homelands with a better and everlasting abode in Paradise.

Leaving one's home, community, and the familiar can be an overwhelming and deeply painful experience, often leaving scars that last a lifetime.

For many trauma survivors, the loss of home is not just physical but a deep soul ache. It is profoundly comforting to remember that many of the Prophets themselves endured exile and displacement. This shared experience connects us to their strength and reminds us of the immense reward Allah has prepared for those who endure the hardship of forced migration with patience and faith.

Just as you take care of your home in this life, how can you beautify your eternal home?

58. Sponsor Orphans

Chapter 4, Verse 2 (Give orphans their wealth)

Allah cares deeply for orphans, warning those who treat them harshly and giving glad tidings to those who care for them with kindness and compassion.

War is brutal and devastating, and children are often the invisible victims, bearing the heaviest burdens of conflicts started by adults, losing their families, homes, and sense of safety in the process. The trauma experienced by orphans is profound, as they face not only the loss of loved ones but also the challenge of navigating a world that may feel uncertain.

Islam places great emphasis on treating orphans with grace, encouraging the community to support and sponsor them whenever possible.

Honor yourself or someone you love by sponsoring an orphan, if you are able to do so.

59. Focus on the Positive

Chapter 4, Verse 19 (You may hate something which Allah turns into a great blessing)

Allah commands us to treat our spouses with grace and reminds us that even if we dislike something about our loved ones, we will find many more things to appreciate and love. When we focus on the negative, small issues become magnified, but when we consciously look for the positive, we will find plenty of reasons to cherish one another.

Trauma can slowly seep into the fabric of this sacred bond, quietly eroding its foundation, creating distance, misunderstanding, and pain. It is vital for spouses to be especially mindful of how trauma, whether personal or shared, can impact their relationship, communication, and emotional wellbeing. By nurturing empathy, patience, and forgiveness, couples can protect and rebuild their connection even in the face of adversity. That in turn would set a healthy example for the children who are watching and who usually learn through modeling.

Write down three positive qualities about your spouse. When you feel frustrated or hurt by them, can you remind yourself of these qualities?

60. Keep Allah in Mind

Chapter 4, Verse 25 (Allah knows best ˹the state of˺ your faith ˹and theirs˺)

Allah knows that human beings are prone to weakness and shortcomings. It is part of our nature to make mistakes and face moments of vulnerability. When we err, it is essential to show sincere remorse, seek forgiveness, and strive to recover quickly.

Grace becomes especially important when working through trauma, as wounds can make us more reactive, fragile, or withdrawn. Embodying grace allows us to move beyond pain, extend compassion to ourselves and others, and rebuild trust.

Before acting on the next impulse, can you pause and ask yourself: "Does this please Allah?"

61. Leave No One Behind

Chapter 4, Verse 29 (And do not kill ⌐each other or⌐ yourselves)

Trauma is a significant risk factor for suicide.

Painful experiences, especially those left unprocessed, can overwhelm the survivor of trauma, leading some to struggle with thoughts of self-harm or despair. There is deep comfort in knowing that Allah sees, hears, and bears witness to even the silent cries of those in pain. He is near to the brokenhearted, and His mercy encompasses all things. In Islam, life is sacred, and taking one's own life is considered a grave sin. However, this does not mean we shame or isolate those who are struggling. Instead, it is a communal obligation to address the root causes of suicide. It takes an entire Ummah to build an environment where no one feels alone, desperate, invisible, or left behind. We must become a safety net, not a source of judgment. May we become the reason someone chooses to hold on, rather than give up.

How would you treat someone wearing a sticker on their heart that reads: "Fragile. Handle with care"?

62. Invitation to Responsibility

Chapter 4, Verse 34 (Men are the caretakers of women)

Allah entrusted men with the responsibility of caring for and protecting women. The Muslim home is meant to be a place of emotional safety, spiritual nourishment, and mutual respect—a sanctuary where both hearts can grow closer to each other and to Allah. Domestic violence has no place in Islam. It directly contradicts the Prophetic model of mercy.

Trauma, especially unaddressed intergenerational or childhood trauma, can show up in marriage through anger, control, emotional shutdown, or avoidance. It can erode the sacred bond between spouses, creating fear instead of trust, and distance instead of closeness. In times of marital discord, Islam encourages reconciliation with grace, patience, and support, not power struggles or emotional harm. Even if healing takes time, reviving one another's soul is a form of worship.

What are three things you are doing intentionally to revive, rather than crush, your spouse's soul? And even if you are single, are you looking after the women in your life?

63. Look Beyond the Sin

Chapter 4, Verse 49 (It is Allah who elevates whoever He wills)

Allah is able to forgive any sin. His door is always open to those who sincerely turn back to Him in repentance. No matter how far someone has strayed, the path to return is never closed, so long as there is breath in the lungs and remorse in the heart. We must be careful not to fall into arrogance or self-righteousness when witnessing others make mistakes. Only Allah knows the secrets of the hearts, the weight of a person's wounds, and the complexity of what they carry.

After trauma, people might fall short of the behaviors expected of them. They may become reactive, withdrawn, or make choices that are misaligned with their values, not out of defiance, but as a cry for help. Instead of harsh judgment or anger, Islam teaches us to show compassion, to be curious and caring rather than furious and condemning, and to walk beside people on the road back to Allah. Be humble. It is the mercy of Allah that our private sins are not publicly displayed. Remember that a bad deed that brings you closer to Allah is better than a good deed that takes you away from Him.

How do you cover the faults of others and gently hold their hand back toward Allah?

64. Never Betray Trust

Chapter 4, Verse 58 (Indeed, Allah commands you to return trusts to their rightful owners)

Allah commands us to keep our promises and never betray the trust others place in us. He also instructs us to judge between people with fairness and integrity, without bias, favoritism, or emotional sway. When we are uncertain or conflicted, we are reminded to return to the ultimate sources of truth and guidance: the Quran and the Sunnah.

This Divine principle has a deep application in the field of trauma. When someone chooses to trust us with their story, especially a story filled with pain, shame, or secrecy, we are being granted a sacred trust. Self-disclosure is not easy; it is often a courageous, vulnerable act. Many trauma survivors have had their voices silenced, their truths denied, or their pain dismissed for many years. To betray that trust, by gossiping, minimizing, invalidating, erasing, or rushing to fix, can be re-traumatizing and deeply wounding.

The next time someone opens up to you, ask yourself if you are holding their story with the care and confidentiality it deserves?

65. Revive the Sunnah

Chapter 4, Verse 65 (But no! By your Lord, they will never be ˹true˺ believers until they accept you as the judge)

When the beloved Prophet was alive, safety was in his shade. Now that he is no longer physically with us, safety and salvation remain in his Sunnah, for those who choose to revive it, live by it, and submit to it with sincerity and love.

The Prophet was not only the final messenger but also the ultimate healer. He endured immense emotional, physical, social, and spiritual pain and still responded with grace.

For trauma survivors, this offers profound comfort. Studying his life and embodying his teachings can help anchor a heart that feels scattered or shattered. Reviving the Sunnah is not just about rituals, it is about returning to a model of embodying his blessed life.

What are three ways you are currently trying to revive the Sunnah?

66. Nothing Without Allah's Permission

Chapter 4, Verse 78 (Both good and evil have been destined by Allah)

Allah promises that His plan will always prevail, no matter how sophisticated or widespread the plots of evil may seem. Falsehood may appear dominant for a time, but it will always be fragile and rotten at its core.

For those healing from trauma, this message is vital. Trauma often leaves behind a lingering sense of powerlessness, especially when the harm came from those in authority, or when justice was denied. It can lead to the belief that evil wins, that darkness is stronger than light, or that hope is futile. But Allah reminds us again and again even when we feel overwhelmed, anxious, or uncertain about the future, our healing begins when we hand over our fear to the One who never abandons us. Trusting Allah with our pain does not erase our wounds, but it gives them meaning and anchors our heart in something more powerful than fear: Divine wisdom.

What are three things you currently fear most? How can you trust Allah with your worries?

67. Allah is Most Powerful

Chapter 4, Verse 84 (And Allah is far superior in might and in punishment)

Allah is fully capable of destroying the mightiest of His enemies without any assistance. Yet, in His infinite wisdom, He invites believers to join His cause to become agents of justice and truth. When they respond to His call with sincerity and steadfastness, He grants them victory, not just in the battlefield, but also in the mending of their hearts.

Trauma can shrink our perspective. It can cloud our ability to see beauty, meaning, or Divine order. For those who have experienced trauma, especially trauma caused by oppression, violence, or betrayal, this Verse offers deep comfort. It reminds us that Allah is never heedless. It is not our strength that brings victory, but our alignment with Allah's will. Even when we feel broken or powerless, we are still invited to be part of something sacred and far greater than ourselves.

How can you use both your heart and mind—your spiritual insight and your senses—to deepen your connection with Allah?

68. Face Allah

Chapter 4, Verse 87 (Allah, there is no god except Him. He will certainly gather you together on the Day of Judgment—about which there is no doubt)

Allah will gather all of His creation and judge between them with perfect justice. Each one of us will meet Allah alone, without our families, titles, or possessions. Meeting our Maker is not a possibility, it is a certainty. What unfolds after that meeting will be shaped by the choices we make today, including how we show up for others, how we heal our world, and how we navigate our wounds.

For those who have experienced trauma, this reminder can feel both heavy and hopeful. Heavy, because trauma can distort our sense of worth, leaving us unsure if we are enough in the eyes of God. Hopeful, because Allah is the Most Just and the Most Merciful, He knows the full story. The tears no one saw. The battles we fought in silence. The good intentions buried under survival mode.

Write a list of answers you would hope to give when you meet your Maker.

69. Life is Sacred

Chapter 4, Verse 92 (It is not lawful for a believer to kill another except by mistake)

One of the first matters Allah will question us about on the Day of Judgment is bloodshed. This shows the immense value Islam places on the sanctity of life. But harm is not limited to physical violence, sometimes words leave deeper wounds than sharp weapons. A harsh comment, a judgmental look, or the spread of harmful gossip can leave emotional scars that last a lifetime.

For trauma survivors, the pain of being shamed, humiliated, dismissed, or silenced can shape how they see themselves and the world. Islam teaches us that the believer is one from whose tongue and hands others feel safe. To meet Allah with a clean record, we must not only avoid direct harm, but also repair the harm we may have caused, intentionally or unintentionally. True God-consciousness requires us to be gentle with people's hearts, knowing we may be touching an already wounded soul.

How do you speak when angry? Have you apologized for past harm? Do your words offer safety or anxiety to others?

70. Be On the Frontlines

Chapter 4, Verse 95 (Those believers who stay at home—except those with valid excuses—are not equal to those who strive in the cause of Allah with their wealth and their lives)

Islam is a religion of action, not just empty words. In the eyes of Allah, those who are on the frontlines, striving for justice and healing, are not equal to those who remain behind without a valid reason. Allah calls us to stand up, serve, and actively participate in bringing goodness to the world.

Even in the aftermath of trauma and devastation, especially in such times, opportunities to serve arise. Whether it is caring for survivors, advocating for the oppressed, feeding the hungry, or simply being a source of comfort to someone in pain, being present and engaged is a form of worship. For trauma survivors, being of service can become part of the healing process. Taking action, no matter how small, can shift the focus from internal chaos to external compassion. It can be deeply grounding to realize: "I still have something to give".

Are you on the frontlines of service?

71. Console Your Soul

Chapter 4, Verse 103 (But when you are secure, establish regular prayers)

Allah commands us to be mindful of our prayers, for prayer truly brings comfort and tranquility to the restless heart and troubled soul.

In the midst of life's chaos and the turmoil caused by trauma, prayer serves as a powerful anchor, grounding us and reconnecting us to the Divine source of peace. Trauma can leave the soul feeling shattered, overwhelmed, and disconnected. In such moments, prayer becomes more than just rituals, it is a lifeline, a safe space where one can pour out pain, seek refuge, and find solace.

When your soul feels restless and weighed down by pain, how do you console it?

72. Be a Healing Source

Chapter 4, Verse 114 (There is no good in most of their secret talks)

Most of our speech is unnecessary except for what encourages charity, acts of kindness, and reconciliation between people.

In a world often marked by conflict and pain, our words have the power to either heal or hurt. What a beautiful legacy it is to be remembered as a source of safety, comfort, and healing for others, especially for those who carry the invisible wounds of trauma. When trauma survivors encounter voices of compassion and understanding, it can help rebuild their trust and sense of safety, which are essential for healing.

What are three ways you serve as a source of healing for those around you?

73. Be Their Voice

Chapter 4, Verse 127 (Also helpless children, as well as standing up for orphans' rights)

Allah speaks up for the voiceless, defending the rights of the oppressed, the invisible, the lonely, the vulnerable, and those living on the margins of society.

As believers, if we truly hold faith in Allah and His Prophet, we must strive to do the same. One of the most beloved deeds in Islam is to speak the truth, even when it is difficult or risky.

For trauma survivors, having someone raise their voice on their behalf can be a powerful step toward regaining their own voice, removing isolation, and restoring dignity. Silence often deepens the wounds of injustice, but courageous advocacy can be a beacon of hope for those who feel unseen and unheard.

What are three ways you are actively speaking up for the voiceless and standing with those who suffer in silence?

74. The Honor is Allah's

Chapter 4, Verse 139 (Surely all honor and power belongs to Allah)

Allah is the ultimate source of dignity and honor. Standing up for justice is one of the most important ways we can earn and preserve that dignity and honor in this life and the next.

For those who have experienced trauma, especially oppression and injustice, reclaiming dignity can be a long and painful journey. Supporting the causes of the oppressed not only helps heal others but also strengthens our own hearts and souls. Even small acts of solidarity like raising awareness, offering support, or speaking out can contribute to restoring justice and healing deep wounds.

How have you supported the causes of the oppressed around the world, within your capacity?

75. The Power is the Believers'

Chapter 4, Verse 141 (And Allah will never grant the disbelievers a way over the believers)

A believer who truly leans on their Lord will never be defeated. This is a Divine promise that we must hold onto firmly, especially during times of hardship when hope feels distant. Victory may not come immediately, but it will come eventually. This is a source of comfort and strength for the wounded.

Trauma can make us feel powerless and isolated, but relying on Allah's support reconnects us to an unshakable power that transcends any worldly setback.

What are three ways you are a source of strength and support for the Ummah?

76. Forgive

Chapter 4, Verse 149 (Allah is Ever-Pardoning, Most Capable)

Allah encourages us to forgive wrongdoing, if we are able. We forgive for His sake, seeking His reward and peace in our hearts. However, forgiveness is a choice, not a Divine mandate forced upon someone, especially not upon those who have been deeply wounded. No one should feel pressured to forgive before they are ready, and religious teachings should never be misused to guilt or shame someone into premature forgiveness.

Trauma can leave deep, invisible scars. For some survivors, forgiving their abuser may bring healing. For others, forgiveness may feel impossible, and that is okay. In such cases, transferring the matter to the "Divine Court", trusting that Allah is the Most Just and Most Aware, can be a profound act of faith. Justice in this life may fail, but Divine justice never does. It is important to honor where you are on your healing journey. Whether you are ready to forgive, are still holding pain, or are seeking forgiveness yourself, acknowledging your emotions is the first step.

Who are three people you would like to forgive or from whom you hope to seek forgiveness?

77. Allah Knows

Chapter 4, Verse 166 (And Allah ˈaloneˈ is sufficient as a Witness)

Some people feel discouraged, or even defeated, when their efforts go unnoticed or unrecognized by others. This can be especially painful for those who already carry wounds from trauma, where being unseen, unheard, or unvalued may echo past experiences of neglect, rejection, or abandonment. But remember: the Quran did not mention the names or stories of many Prophets, yet their honor and rank with Allah remain untouched. Their omission from the narrative is not a reflection of their silence on the ground. Likewise, countless people today do incredible things far from the spotlight. They serve quietly, love deeply, and give generously, not for the applause, but for the pleasure of their Lord. They seek no worldly credit, because they know that Allah sees what others may overlook. If people fail to acknowledge your efforts, know this: Allah knows your heart, your intention, and your sacrifices, and that is enough.

On a piece of paper, write in bold letters: "Allah Knows". Then, pour your heart out to the One who understands what no one else can.

78. Be a Support System

Chapter 5, Verse 2 (Cooperate with one another in goodness and righteousness)

To be expected to do everything, for everyone, all the time, is simply not realistic, nor is it sustainable. This kind of pressure can lead to emotional exhaustion, burnout, and even resentment, especially for those already carrying the invisible weight of trauma. We are not meant to live in isolation. Human beings are social by design. We thrive in healthy relationships, grounded in mutual support, shared responsibility, and collective care. We need a tribe, a safe, compassionate community where burdens are shared and healing is possible.

After trauma, when needs multiply and emotional reserves run low, the path to recovery becomes clearer and more impactful when we collaborate rather than compete. It is not about doing everything alone; it is about doing something together.

How can others experience you as a source of support?

79. Religion of Ease

Chapter 5, Verse 6 (It is not Allah's Will to burden you)

Islam came as a source of ease, not hardship. When religious duties begin to feel like a heavy burden rather than a source of peace, it may be a sign that they are not being approached in the way they were Divinely intended, or that one's emotional and psychological state needs more attention. The beloved Prophet used to find comfort, not distress, in the rituals of worship. His prayers were not a chore, but a refuge. He is reported to have said, "Let us find rest in it, O Bilal", referring to the prayer.

For trauma survivors, acts of worship can sometimes feel triggering, especially when pain, guilt, or burnout distorts one's connection with faith. In such cases, it is crucial to return to the spirit of Islam: one of compassion, healing, and Divine understanding. Islam does not ignore our struggles, it embraces them. Religious practices should be a pathway to healing, not a cause for shame, and Allah, in His infinite mercy, meets each person where they are.

Do you currently view your duties as a Muslim as a source of hardship or ease?

80. Navigate Hurt

Chapter 5, Verse 32 (And whoever saves a life, it will be as if they saved all of humanity)

In Islam, human life is sacred. Allah tells us in the Quran that taking one innocent life is like taking the life of all humanity, and saving one life is like saving all of humanity. This sacredness applies to every soul, regardless of background. But when someone is on the receiving end of oppression, violence, or injustice, it can be incredibly difficult to continue seeing others' lives as sacred, especially the lives of those who caused harm. This is a real and valid struggle, particularly for survivors of trauma. Trauma can cloud the heart, distort trust, and trigger deep anger and the desire for retaliation. However, Islam does not call for mass punishment, nor does it condone collective revenge. The Prophet consistently demonstrated restraint, mercy, and justice, even toward his enemies. He acted from a place of moral clarity, not emotional reactivity. Yet, this level of grace requires spiritual maturity, emotional healing, and strong conviction. It is not weakness to feel rage or hurt, it is human. But it is strength to seek healing, and to respond in a way that upholds the dignity of all of Allah's creation.

Are you treating all of Allah's creation as sacred? What about those who have wronged you?

81. Uphold Justice

Chapter 5, Verse 42 (Surely Allah loves those who are just)

To judge between people should always be done through justice, guided by the Quran and Sunnah. When individuals deviate from Divine guidance as the final authority in matters of conflict, relationships, or rulings, they risk falling into oppression and wrongdoing, knowingly or unknowingly. In Islam, justice is not optional; it is a sacred mandate.

But what happens when trauma clouds our clarity? After traumatic experiences, whether personal or collective, our ability to remain neutral and just can be compromised. Emotional wounds, unresolved pain, or biased loyalties can lead us to rush to conclusions, project our own fears, or side with those who mirror our pain. This is understandable, but not always fair. Justice is essential not only for society to function, but for true, meaningful healing to take place. For a traumatized heart to feel safe again, it must believe that fairness still exists, that people will be heard, and that the wronged will be seen. That is why Islam centers justice, even if it is against our own selves or our closest loved ones.

Recall the last time you were asked to judge between people. Did you do that fairly?

82. Do Not Get Replaced

Chapter 5, Verse 54 (O believers! Whoever among you abandons their faith, Allah will replace them with others who love Him and are loved by Him)

A believer who abandons their faith harms no one but themselves. If we turn away from Allah, He does not lose anything, but we risk losing everything. The Quran reminds us that if we fail to live up to our role, Allah will replace us with those more sincere, more compassionate, and more committed.

The wounds of trauma are not signs of weakness or rejection. They are Divine invitations. Invitations from Allah to rise, to reflect, and to care for His creation with deeper empathy and understanding. Often, those who have tasted pain become the most powerful healers and advocates, if they do not turn away. When trauma is not addressed, it can lead to spiritual numbness, withdrawal from religious practices, or even questioning one's worth in the eyes of Allah. But healing does not mean pretending we are fine, it means showing up sincerely, even when we feel broken. It means doing Allah's work with whatever strength we have left.

What are three things you are actively doing to not get replaced by Allah?

83. Never Start Fires

Chapter 5, Verse 64 (Whenever they kindle the fire of war, Allah puts it out)

There are some people who love to ignite fires, whether through spreading rumors, stirring division, or causing corruption in their communities. They may appear powerful in the moment, but Allah warns that He will extinguish every single fire they start.

This Divine promise is deeply comforting, especially for those who have been burned by the fires of betrayal, abuse, and injustice. When someone intentionally wounds us, emotionally, spiritually, or physically, it can feel like that fire will never go out. But Allah is the one who gives healing, justice, and restoration in ways we may not see immediately, but which always come in due time. Knowing that Allah can extinguish both external conflict and the internal flames of trauma can help survivors feel safer, grounded, and less alone.

Do you start, feed, or extinguish fires around you?

84. Safeguard Blessings

Chapter 5, Verse 66 (They would have been overwhelmed with provisions from above and below)

Allah opens the doors of His blessings to those who show sincere gratitude. When we begin to take His favors for granted and fall into a state of ingratitude, we risk losing those blessings altogether.

For those of us who work with trauma survivors, it is humbling to witness their deep appreciation for even the smallest of blessings. Despite their pain, loss, and limited resources, many of them display a remarkable willingness to give, to smile, and to express thanks, while asking for nothing in return. Gratitude, in this context, becomes an act of resistance against hopelessness and despair. For trauma survivors, finding something to be grateful for, no matter how small, can be a powerful tool in their healing journey. It shifts the focus from what is broken to what still remains, even if it is only a flicker of light.

Look closely at the blessings Allah has given you. Are you using these gifts to bring healing or harm?

85. Change Evil

Chapter 5, Verse 79 (They did not forbid one another from doing evil)

Allah curses those who witness evil and remain silent or passive, those who neither try to change it with their hands, nor speak out against it with their tongues, nor even reject it in their hearts. Oppression, injustice, and abuse are among the most destructive forms of evil. They strip individuals of their dignity, silence their voices, and leave deep psychological wounds that can last a lifetime.

Trauma survivors often report not only the pain of what happened to them, but also the pain of being ignored, dismissed, or abandoned by those who saw and did nothing. Remaining silent in the face of harm, especially systemic harm or repeated patterns of abuse, can re-traumatize those who are already suffering and signal that their lives do not matter. Silence is not neutrality, it is complicity.

Think of an injustice or act of evil happening around you right now, whether it is in your home, your community, or on the global stage. Have you tried to stop it with whatever means available to you?

86. Do Not Transgress

Chapter 5, Verse 87 (And do not transgress. Indeed, Allah does not like transgressors)

Throughout the Quran, Allah repeatedly warns us against transgression—going beyond the limits set by Him. Transgression is among the gravest sins because it violates the rights of others, often causing deep, lasting harm, sometimes trauma that scars a person's heart and soul indefinitely.

When boundaries are crossed, whether in relationships, communities, or society, it can lead to feelings of betrayal, helplessness, and ongoing emotional wounding. For trauma survivors, respecting boundaries is essential for healing and safety.

Take time to clearly outline the personal boundaries that you need for your own healing and wellbeing. Do you respect the boundaries of others in return?

87. Watch Your Alone Time

Chapter 5, Verse 94 (To distinguish those who fear Him in secret)

Allah tells us that there will come a time when evil becomes so widespread and easily accessible that obtaining it requires little to no effort. For example, accessing harmful websites can happen with just the touch of a finger. This serves as a test for those who keep Allah in their minds and hearts, not only in public but also in private, behind closed doors.

Impulsive and risky behaviors are often expressions of a restless soul seeking relief, especially after trauma. Such actions may be misguided attempts to soothe deep emotional pain or numb overwhelming feelings. Instead of being furious or punishing these behaviors, it is more effective to be curious about the underlying wounds and trauma that fuel them, and to seek healing from the root causes.

Imagine the Prophet is about to enter your room or check your phone. Would you do anything differently?

88. Be Exceptional

Chapter 5, Verse 100 (Say, ˈO Prophet,ˈ "Good and evil are not equal, though you may be dazzled by the abundance of evil")

Good and evil will never be equal, even if evil becomes widespread and seems to dominate. Just because something is popular or attractive does not make it right or beneficial to follow or attach to.

After trauma, some people may cope by blindly following trends, even when those behaviors conflict with their pre-trauma values and deeply held beliefs. This can be a way to find belonging or numb pain, but it may lead them further away from healing and true purpose.

What are three trends or influences you currently follow? How do they align, or conflict, with your values and beliefs?

89. Believe Unconditionally

Chapter 5, Verse 113 (To verify you are indeed truthful to us)

Belief is a matter of the heart. We should have faith and certainty in Allah, even when we do not fully understand the "bigger picture".

This can be especially difficult to grasp after experiencing trauma. Many people struggle with questions like, "Why do bad things happen to good people?" Such questions deserve compassion, thoughtful reflection, and open discussion, not shaming or dismissal. Trauma can shake our faith, leaving us feeling lost and doubtful, but it also offers an opportunity to deepen our trust in Allah's wisdom, even amid uncertainty.

Do you find yourself worshiping Allah conditionally? How can you nurture a heart that trusts Allah unconditionally, even in the darkest moments?

90. Mercy is His Essence

Chapter 6, Verse 12 (He has taken upon Himself to be Merciful)

Allah chose mercy to be His very essence. He tests us with both what we love and what we fear or dislike. Whatever He decrees will inevitably happen, even if we do not understand it in the moment. Eventually, everything Allah decrees is a form of mercy.

After trauma, it can be difficult to recognize Allah's mercy. Pain and suffering often cloud our hearts and minds. Yet, the beauty of Allah's mercy is subtle and profound, like a breathtaking rainbow that appears after a heavy storm, reminding us that light always follows darkness.

Draw a rainbow that follows heavy rain. Can you still find traces of beauty after something "ugly"?

91. Take Advantage of Today

Chapter 6, Verse 27 (Oh! If only we could be sent back)

On their deathbed, many people wish they had more time or a second chance to make things right. We are blessed to still be here, given the opportunity to strive harder, because tomorrow is never guaranteed. Tomorrow is the day when we will face the results of our actions. No matter what has happened, we can all do better, starting now.

After trauma, it is especially important to help ourselves and others stay grounded in the present moment, in the "here-and-now", to find a sense of safety and stability amid the chaos of past pain and future uncertainty.

If you were given a second chance at life after death, what would you do differently?

92. Even Prophets Faced Rejection

Chapter 6, Verse 34 (Indeed, messengers before you were rejected)

In many places in the Quran, Allah reminds our beloved Prophet not to grieve over those who reject the message. Throughout history, many nations have rejected their Prophets, despite their sincere efforts to guide and heal their communities. Guidance is ultimately in the hands of Allah, and our responsibility is to convey the message and embody it, not to force it upon others.

The trauma of rejection can deeply wound our sense of worth and self-esteem, often leaving us feeling isolated and misunderstood. It is important to remember that rejection usually says more about the pain of those who reject than about the one who is rejected. For survivors of trauma, rejection can reopen old wounds, making it harder to trust and feel vulnerable.

Take time to study the stories of three Prophets who were rejected by their people.

93. Allah is Never Heedless

Chapter 6, Verse 38 (We have left nothing out of the Record)

This Verse was the inspiration behind writing this book. Allah tells us that He has included everything we need in His Book: guidance, wisdom, and healing. I wondered if I would find tools for healing trauma within the Quran, and indeed, I discovered that the Quran holds profound remedies for the wounds of the heart and soul.

Trauma can leave us feeling lost, broken, and desperate for healing. The Quran offers comfort, strength, and practical guidance to help us rebuild ourselves and others after trauma.

Take a moment to reflect on three challenges currently affecting you, your family, your community, the Ummah, or even all of humanity. Then, explore how the Quran provides healing tools for each of these struggles.

94. Company Matters

Chapter 6, Verse 52 (ʿO Prophet!ʾ Do not dismiss those ʿpoor believersʾ who invoke their Lord)

The rich and powerful demanded that the Prophet exclude the poor as a condition to listen to his message. Yet, Allah commanded His beloved Prophet to spend even more time with those who are often invisible and marginalized. Sometimes, those whom society looks down upon are the closest to Allah.

One act of service deeply cherished by the Prophet was sitting with trauma survivors, wiping their tears, comforting their hearts, and nursing their wounds with compassion and care. Trauma often isolates people, making them feel unseen and forgotten. In a world that ignores their pain, your presence and kindness can be a powerful source of hope and healing.

Do you seek out those whom others ignore or avoid?

95. Nothing is Haphazard

Chapter 6, Verse 59 (With Him are the keys of the unseen—no one knows them except Him)

With so much trauma and suffering happening throughout the world, many may find themselves asking, "Where is Allah in all of this?"

Allah reassures the hearts of His servants that He is always watching, listening, and fully aware of every act of injustice and pain. Nothing escapes His knowledge or sight. Though we may not see immediate change, Allah will intervene and bring justice at the time He wills, perfectly and beyond our limited understanding.

What are three questions people commonly ask about Allah in the aftermath of trauma?

96. Seek Allah

Chapter 6, Verse 76 (This is my Lord!)

When Prophet Abraham was searching for his Lord, he sought beauty, light, and magnificence; all are signs of the Divine presence.

Similarly, when we seek Allah, especially after experiencing trauma, we can find Him reflected in the small acts of beauty and kindness around us. Trauma often exposes both the darkest and brightest aspects of the human spirit. It challenges us but also offers a rare opportunity to choose healing over harm and compassion over bitterness. If you decide to heal rather than hurt yourself and others, you are walking the path toward recognizing the Divine light within and around you.

What did Prophet Abraham look for when searching for Allah?

97. The Bedrock of Safety

Chapter 6, Verse 82 (It is ˹only˺ those who are faithful and do not tarnish their faith with falsehood who are guaranteed security and are ˹rightly˺ guided)

Those who believe and do not wrong themselves through injustice will attain safety and guidance. Justice is a profound and beautiful attribute of Allah, reflecting His perfect balance with mercy.

Pursuing justice is essential, not only in faith but also as a crucial step toward finding meaning, closure, and healing after trauma. Without justice, healing remains incomplete. Trauma healing must honor and restore justice to truly support survivors. Injustice deepens wounds and perpetuates pain, while justice offers a path to restoration and peace.

Take time to research the virtue of justice in the life of the Prophet and his four rightly guided caliphs.

98. Share Your Light

Chapter 6, Verse 122 (Can those who had been dead, to whom We gave life and a light with which they can walk among people, be compared to those in complete darkness from which they can never emerge?)

Allah wants us to abandon all sins so that we may find His radiant light inside each one of us. When we find Allah's light, it becomes our duty to share it with His creation, especially those walking through the darkness of pain.

After trauma, many feel broken, lost, or beyond repair, but Allah's light reminds us that healing is always possible. To glimpse His light shining through the shadows of suffering is a profound sign of strength. This light can gently guide wounded hearts toward mending, even when the weight of trauma feels unbearable.

What are three sources of light within you that you intend to share with others? How can you protect, nurture, and brighten the light in your heart?

99. Absolute Justice

Chapter 6, Verse 131 (Your Lord would never destroy a society for their wrongdoing while its people are unaware ˹of the truth˺)

Out of His infinite mercy, Allah never punishes a town or a nation without first sending warnings and giving them many chances to repent and change their ways.

For those who suffer oppression and injustice, this is a source of deep comfort and hope: knowing that Allah is fully aware of their pain and will ultimately hold the arrogant oppressors accountable. Even when trauma and suffering seem endless, Allah's mercy means there is always an opportunity for healing. This reminder encourages patience and trust in Divine justice, even when human systems fail to deliver it.

Can you reflect on Allah's mercy in giving His creation repeated chances to correct their path?

100. Allah's True Promise

Chapter 6, Verse 134 (Indeed, what you have been promised will certainly come to pass)

Allah is not in need of His servants, yet He is the very embodiment of infinite mercy. When His servants turn away from Him, Allah can easily replace them with others who remain steadfast.

After experiencing trauma, it is common for people to ask, "Why me?", struggling to understand their suffering. Yet on the Day of Judgment, those very souls will wish they had endured even greater trials when they witness the immense reward Allah has prepared for the patient and faithful. A true believer embraces the Divine decree with a humble "Why not me?", welcoming whatever their Maker has destined, trusting in His wisdom and mercy.

Reflect on three ways Allah's promise of mercy and justice has come true in your life.

101. Oppression Misguides

Chapter 6, Verse 144 (Surely Allah does not guide the wrongdoing people)

When the Children of Israel questioned every small detail and challenged Allah's authority, they made things unnecessarily difficult for themselves. In contrast, the Ummah of Prophet Muhammad is blessed with listening and obeying—a beautiful expression of submission and trust in Divine wisdom. Oppression is one of the gravest spiritual and moral failures. Those who transgress against others, shedding innocent blood or silencing the vulnerable, may appear powerful, but they are in fact deeply blinded. Their injustice not only harms others, but it also veils their connection to their Lord and corrodes their souls from within.

For trauma survivors, witnessing or experiencing oppression can shake the foundations of faith. It is valid to feel confused, angry, or even distant from religion after such experiences. But part of reclaiming your spiritual healing is recognizing that Islam stands firmly against all forms of injustice, no matter who commits it.

What does it really mean to be a Muslim? Remember that oppression can contradict the very essence of belief.

102. Devote

Chapter 6, Verse 162 (Say, "Surely my prayer, my sacrifice, my life, and my death are all for Allah—Lord of all worlds")

Dealing with Allah always means winning. When we devote all of our affairs—our fears, our hopes, our actions, and our relationships, to pleasing Allah, we place ourselves on the path of His Divine pleasure and our ultimate success.

In times of collective trauma, like the dark days we are witnessing across the Ummah, our connection to Allah becomes even more critical. Trauma can make people feel abandoned, unsafe, and powerless. But turning back to the One who never leaves, who sees and hears all, is how we begin to heal, both individually and as a community.

Draw three circles closest to your heart. Draw lines connecting each of them to Allah.

103. Injustice Equals Losing

Chapter 7, Verse 9 (But those whose scale is light, they have doomed themselves for wrongfully denying Our signs)

Engaging in injustice causes deep corruption in this life and can be a major reason for losing out on the joys of the next. While an oppressor might sleep soundly under the illusion that Allah is unaware or indifferent, the oppressed often lie awake—grieving, hurting, but holding onto the certainty of Allah's ultimate justice. This contrast is a powerful reminder: What matters most is not who seems to win today, but who will stand victorious tomorrow, on the Day when all hidden truths are revealed and every injustice is accounted for.

Which of your deeds are heavy on the scale of the hereafter?

104. The Price of Arrogance

Chapter 7, Verse 13 (So get out! You are truly one of the disgraced)

Satan made a vow to lead humankind away from the straight path. His most effective weapon is to distract us from expressing gratitude to our Lord.

When we experience trauma, especially in its early stages, we may become vulnerable to these whispers. Pain can distort our perception of reality, and the inner voice of despair may begin to sound like truth. In such moments, it becomes easier to question, doubt, and even lose sight of Divine mercy. The devil exploits this vulnerability, trying to make us feel abandoned, unloved, or rejected, rather than supported, guided, and held. That is why social support is vital after trauma. The right company can become our tribe that shields us against the evil tricks and weapons of the devil.

How can gratitude be an effective shield against the wounds of trauma?

105. Let Go of Hatred

Chapter 7, Verse 43 (We will remove whatever bitterness they had in their hearts)

In Paradise, the believers will have no hatred, envy, or ill feelings toward one another. That state of peace is a reflection of whom they chose to be in this life. They learned to forgive, to overlook mistakes, and to rise above the things that drain their energy and distract their hearts. These qualities are often easier to embody during times of ease, but after trauma, especially when emotions are raw and wounds are fresh, holding onto noble character becomes much harder. Pain can cloud our judgment, and the instinct to protect ourselves can sometimes lead us to hold onto anger, resentment, or distrust, thinking it keeps us safe. This is where faith becomes a compass. It reminds us that healing and strength do not come from holding grudges but from surrendering the weight that holds us down to the only One who can carry it.

Hatred is a heavy weight that pulls people down and can keep them stuck. What would it take to begin releasing hatred from your heart?

106. Do Not Take Part in Corruption

Chapter 7, Verse 56 (Do not spread corruption in the land after it has been set in order)

Allah wants us to engage in grace and in building people up, not in evil and tearing them down. Believers are called to be sources of healing, even when they themselves are hurting.

Even after experiencing trauma, we are encouraged to resist the temptation to spread harm, because hurting others does not heal our wounds. Islam teaches us that trauma is never a justification for cruelty. It is a test, and with that test comes a choice: to perpetuate the cycle of pain or to interrupt it.

Words and actions are your gifts to people. How can you ensure your gifts are wrapped in grace?

107. Plant Your Seeds

Chapter 7, Verse 58 (The fertile land produces abundantly by the Will of its Lord, whereas the infertile land hardly produces anything)

Good seeds, when planted in good soil, produce good fruits. To build a strong, compassionate society, especially for our future generations, we must embody the beauty of Islam through our actions, not just our words. When we walk the talk, we become living proof of Divine guidance.

But life can test even the best of us. When our basic needs, like safety, stability, or belonging, are threatened, especially after trauma, we may fall short. We might react in ways that do not align with our values. We might speak harshly, withdraw, or act out of fear or pain. In those moments, it is essential to acknowledge what is happening inside us, give ourselves grace, and commit to repair, with ourselves, with others, and with Allah.

How can you make it a habit to plant good seeds wherever you go? Have the intention that even if you do not see the results, someone, someday, will eat from the fruit of what you have planted.

108. Islam Comes First

Chapter 7, Verse 71 (Do you dispute with me regarding the so-called gods which you and your forefathers have made up)

Islam teaches us to evaluate traditions through the lens of Divine guidance. We are encouraged to follow only what aligns with our faith, even if it means unlearning inherited beliefs, customs, or practices that contradict our religion. This can be especially difficult when culture and identity are deeply intertwined. But truth must take precedence over tradition. The Prophet set a powerful example: he challenged deeply rooted cultural norms of his time like tribalism, injustice, racism, and patriarchy, not out of rebellion, but out of a higher loyalty to Allah. Much of the pain we witness in the world like wars, oppression, and cycles of violence, can be traced back to unhealed wounds passed down generations. These wounds are often embedded in cultural memory, fueled by a sense of historical grief. Generational trauma is real. But just as trauma can be inherited, so can healing. True healing can start when we courageously say: "This may be what I was taught, but it is not what Islam teaches".

Research how the Prophet prioritized religion over culture.

109. Stand Out

Chapter 7, Verse 82 (They are a people who wish to remain chaste!)

You do not have to give up your moral values or high standards to fit in. Sometimes, the only "crime" people see in you is that you are different, that you do not conform, and that you hold onto your ethics, your modesty, your beliefs, or your identity. That is okay. You were never meant to be a copy. Islam teaches us to stand out, with integrity, with light, and with conviction. But standing out, especially in a world that often misunderstands or vilifies Muslims, can feel isolating, even dangerous. When people call you names, mock your faith, or treat you as "less than" because of your identity, it deeply hurts. This kind of social rejection and identity-based trauma can leave long-lasting emotional scars, and yet Islam teaches us that our worth does not come from people's acceptance, it rather comes from Allah's pleasure. You are sacred for being different. Prophets were seen as "outsiders", and yet, they changed the world.

What are three beautiful qualities that set you apart as a believer? Write them down. Honor them. Protect them.

110. Make Meaning

Chapter 7, Verse 94 (Whenever We sent a Prophet to a society, We afflicted its ʿdisbelievingʾ people with suffering and adversity, so perhaps they would be humbled)

When we are tested with trials, tribulations, or even calamities, our safest response is to run toward Allah, not away from Him. Like fire that refines gold, a test has the power to purify, elevate, and transform. But let us be honest — hardship does not always feel like purification. It can feel crushing, disorienting, and lonely. The real test of character is not in our ease, but in how we respond when everything is falling apart.

For trauma survivors, that response might be silence, withdrawal, anger, numbness, or questioning everything, even Allah's wisdom. After trauma, people often ask "Why me?", "Where was Allah when it happened?", "What did I do to deserve this?". These questions are valid. They are not signs of weak faith; they are part of the meaning-making process. In fact, reflecting on what happened, in a safe and supportive space, is a key part of healing.

Name three Prophets who were heavily tested. Then study their stories.

111. Punishment Comes Suddenly

Chapter 7, Verse 99 (None would feel secure from Allah's planning except the losers)

Allah does not punish sins immediately. Instead, He gives us many chances and opportunities for us to repent, seek forgiveness, and redeem ourselves. When we refuse these invitations, we are the ones who suffer, for our own souls bear the weight of that rejection.

For those who endure injustice and oppression, it can be painfully difficult to trust in Divine justice, especially when it seems delayed. Yet, they can find comfort in knowing that Allah never forgets, and ultimate justice will come in its perfect time, even if it is not to our satisfaction. After trauma, faith can be shaken deeply. The wounds of injustice, betrayal, and loss may lead to spiritual confusion and doubt. It is important to recognize that losing faith temporarily or struggling with belief is a natural response to trauma, not a failure. Healing the heart and restoring trust in Allah often requires time, support, and gentle reminders of His mercy.

What are three things that can destroy faith, especially after trauma? How can you nurture your faith even when your heart feels heavy?

112. Etiquettes of Victory

Chapter 7, Verse 129 (Perhaps your Lord will destroy your enemy and make you successors in the land to see what you will do)

Allah tests people through power shifts to see who truly fulfills their responsibilities. When given a position of authority or privilege, the greatest act of strength is to use that advantage to lift others up, not to push them down. Grace in the face of power is a profound sign of inner strength.

This serves as a powerful reminder for trauma survivors who may have the chance to seek revenge or retaliate against their abusers. No matter how deep our pain runs, we have the right to seek justice, but we also have the power to make the choice to break the cycle of harm by not inflicting pain on others. Choosing mercy and restraint can be a vital step in healing, not just for ourselves, but also for our communities. After trauma, the urge for revenge and retaliation is natural and understandable. Trauma wounds often cry out for recognition and fairness. However, responding with grace and compassion, especially when you hold power, can transform pain into healing and break patterns of violence.

Write a list of things most people do when they gain victory over their "enemies".

113. Happy Ending

Chapter 7, Verse 137 ('In this way' the noble Word of your Lord was fulfilled for the Children of Israel for what they had endured)

History reminds us that tyrants die, empires crumble, and power shifts in the blink of an eye. No matter how permanent or overwhelming oppression may seem, everything is ultimately under Allah's control. Allah alone decides the time, place, and conditions of victory. Our role is to remain steadfast and do our part, no matter how small it may seem.

For those who have suffered under tyranny, injustice, or conflict, it can feel like hope is lost forever. Trauma often distorts time and magnifies pain, making victory seem impossible or far away. Yet, history and the Divine promise remind us that oppression is never permanent. Even the darkest chapters have an end. Reflecting on moments like the conquest of Makkah, where justice was restored, enemies were forgiven, and mercy prevailed, can inspire trauma survivors to hold on to hope.

Reflect on the story of the Conquest of Makkah.

114. Path Towards Paradise

Chapter 7, Verse 142 (Do what is right, and do not follow the way of the corruptors)

When you visit someone who is sick, care for those in need, and handle broken hearts with tenderness and compassion, that is when you truly see Allah in this life and be among those who will see Him in the next.

In moments of suffering, people often feel isolated, forgotten, and invisible. Your acts of kindness become a lifeline, a reminder that Allah's mercy is present even in the darkest times. For survivors of trauma, the smallest gestures of care can mean the world, offering them comfort when the world feels cold and uncaring. These moments of human connection heal wounds that words alone cannot reach. By embodying compassion, you not only ease others' pain but also draw closer to Allah's mercy and presence.

Reflect on Allah's beautiful invitation: "If you had visited My sick servant, you would have found Me there".

115. Injustice Invalidates Deeds

Chapter 7, Verse 146 (I will turn away from My signs those who act unjustly with arrogance in the land)

Arrogance can cause the son of Adam to turn away from his Lord. The greatest punishment, both in this life and the hereafter, is to be distant from Allah.

During times of trauma, it can be difficult to recognize the blessing in not being the perpetrator of harm. Amid the chaos and pain, it may seem easier to blame ourselves or others, but standing firm on the side of justice is a quiet victory. When the dust settles, it brings deep comfort to know you remained on the right side of history. Trauma can sometimes feed arrogance, whether through bitterness, self-righteousness, or the desire to control or dominate to protect oneself. Yet arrogance blinds the heart, distancing it from Allah's mercy and guidance. The healing journey calls for recognition of our vulnerabilities, mistakes, and the need for Allah's grace.

Name three harmful consequences of arrogance. Remember that arrogance can veil you from Allah's presence and mercy.

116. Avoid Fitnah

Chapter 7, Verse 155 (Will You destroy us for what the foolish among us have done?)

Fitnah is a fire that can destroy us, as individuals, families, communities, and even as an Ummah.

In times of mass trauma, such as armed conflicts and forced displacement, people often face many forms of fitnah that can deeply shake their foundational values and core beliefs. The chaos and pain of trauma make us vulnerable to confusion, division, and despair. One important way to protect ourselves from this destructive fire is to avoid engaging in corrupt actions and harmful speech. Our words and deeds carry weight, especially during times of crisis, and they can either fuel the fitnah or help contain it. Trauma can weaken the heart and can cloud judgment, making it easier to fall into anger, suspicion, or bitterness. In these moments, fitnah—whether through rumors, false accusations, or betrayal—can spread rapidly, fracturing trust and safety. Recognizing this vulnerability helps us choose patience, forgiveness, and truth as shields against the fires of fitnah.

Name three ways you can avoid engaging in fitnah.

117. Man is His Own Enemy

Chapter 7, Verse 160 (They ˹certainly˺ did not wrong Us, but wronged themselves)

Transgressing the boundaries set by religion exposes nations to Allah's wrath and risks their destruction. In every moment, we face a profound choice: to cause wounds or to heal them. This choice is ours alone to make. No evil we commit can harm Allah in the least, but our actions carry weight for ourselves.

After trauma, when pain and anger run deep, this choice becomes even more critical. We may feel tempted to lash out or seek revenge, but true healing and self-respect come from choosing the path of righteousness and mercy, even when it is the road less traveled. Trauma can challenge our sense of self-worth and shake our moral compass. But reclaiming our dignity starts with recognizing the power of our choices. When we choose to honor boundaries, both Divine and personal, we begin to mend our wounds and restore the trust broken by suffering.

List three things that help you earn self-respect. Is obedience to Allah at the top of your list?

118. In Allah's Hands

Chapter 7, Verse 188 (Say, "I have no power to benefit or protect myself, except by the Will of Allah")

Man does not have the power to benefit or harm anyone except by the permission of Allah.

When facing trauma, it is natural to feel overwhelmed, powerless, or confused about why certain hardships happen. Yet, reflecting on the vastness of Allah's creation and His perfect management of all affairs can bring deep comfort and reassurance. In moments of trauma, we may struggle to trust that there is a greater plan or purpose behind our suffering. But recognizing that the same Allah who sustains the universe also holds your life and healing in His hands can be a source of profound peace. This understanding invites us to lean into trust and patience, even when the pain feels unbearable.

Look around at all of Allah's creation. How can you rest assured that He is fully capable of managing your affairs, including your healing journey?

119. Stay Focused

Chapter 7, Verse 199 (Be gracious, enjoin what is right, and turn away from those who act arrogantly)

Islam calls us to live a meaningful life, staying true to the purpose for which we were created.

Trauma can shake us deeply, pulling us away from the straight path and leading us toward dangerous detours. When we lose our way, it is important to remember that the door of mercy is always open, and we are always welcome to return. Healing begins the moment we choose to refocus on our ultimate goal—Paradise, and let go of the distractions that pull us away. This redirection is a powerful act of faith and a step closer to healing.

Draw a bull's eye with Paradise at the center. How do you stay focused on your goal?

120. Unavoidable Conflicts

Chapter 8, Verse 5 (When your Lord brought you ˹O Prophet˺ out of your home for a just cause, a group of believers was totally against it)

Fighting, even for a just cause, is rarely something people look forward to. Yet, standing against oppression is sometimes necessary to establish justice and protect the vulnerable.

For trauma survivors, conflict can reopen wounds or trigger feelings of fear and helplessness. Still, resisting injustice is a powerful act of courage. When trauma has already shaken our sense of safety, the idea of fighting, whether literal or metaphorical, can feel overwhelming or frightening. But sometimes, standing firm against oppression is what leads to true healing, not only for ourselves but for entire communities.

Think of three things you initially disliked or resisted but later realized were ultimately for your best interest.

121. Stay the Course

Chapter 8, Verse 11 (Strengthen your hearts, and make ˹your˺ steps firm)

Allah provides many tools to help us remain steadfast. These include faith in His Divine promises, following the Prophetic traditions, studying history, and other more subtle forms of support such as the presence of angels and the blessing of rain.

For those who have endured trauma, steadfastness is especially vital. Trauma can shake our sense of security and hope, making it hard to stay firm in faith. Yet, Allah's tools are designed to strengthen our hearts and remind us that we are never alone in our struggles. After trauma, feelings of doubt, fear, or despair can overwhelm us, but holding onto faith in Allah's promises and drawing strength from the Prophetic example can guide us back to stability. Just as rain nourishes dry land, these supports refresh our spirit and help us grow despite the hardships.

Think of three things that help you stay steadfast when facing adversity.

122. Do Not Turn Away

Chapter 8, Verse 20 (Obey Allah and His Messenger and do not turn away from him while you hear ˹his call)

Allah asks us to respond sincerely to Him and His Prophet. When we hear the Divine call, our hearts should say, "We listen and we obey". This response is what truly revives and strengthens our hearts, especially during difficult times.

After trauma, people's footing can feel slippery. Everyone responds differently. Some may withdraw; others may feel lost or angry. In these moments, it is crucial to approach ourselves and others with curiosity and compassion, rather than judgment or impatience. Trauma can cloud our ability to hear and respond to Allah's call clearly. Healing often requires patience as we navigate pain and uncertainty. Saying "we listen and we obey" is an act of surrender that brings peace and renewal, even when the path feels unclear.

How can you prepare your heart and mind to respond immediately and sincerely when you hear the next call from Allah and His Prophet?

123. The Two Safety Sources

Chapter 8, Verse 33 (But Allah would never punish them while you ˹O Prophet˺ were in their midst. Nor would He ever punish them if they prayed for forgiveness)

This Ummah is blessed with many sources of safety and healing. In times of fear and uncertainty, especially during moments of collective trauma, we need to return to and reconnect with these sources. Two of the most powerful tools for safety are following the way of the Prophet and seeking forgiveness from Allah.

Trauma can make fear feel overwhelming and cause despair about the future of the Ummah. But turning back to the Prophet's example reminds us of patience and unwavering trust in Allah's plan. Seeking forgiveness cleanses the heart, lightens the soul, and opens the door to Divine protection.

When you fear for the Ummah, can you make it a daily habit to follow the example of the Prophet and seek forgiveness from Allah?

124. Invest in What Matters

Chapter 8, Verse 36 (Surely the disbelievers spend their wealth to hinder others from the Path of Allah)

There are those who spend their time, energy, and resources on wickedness and harmful pursuits. None of that will benefit them on the Day of Judgment, when good is clearly distinguished from evil, and when the wicked face the consequences of their actions in the Hellfire.

During times of hardship, disasters, and mass trauma, the Ummah must carefully reflect on where it invests its human and material resources. Trauma often reveals who truly benefits the community and who drains it. It also challenges us to prioritize what brings lasting benefits, rather than temporary gains. Trauma can cause confusion, making it harder to see the path forward clearly. However, it also offers an opportunity for deep reflection on our values and priorities. In moments of crisis, investing in healing, support, and justice creates ripples of restoration that strengthen the Ummah for generations to come.

Take a moment to examine your investments. What are you investing in for the hereafter?

125. Division Causes Defeat

Chapter 8, Verse 46 (Do not dispute with one another, or you would be discouraged and weakened)

The devil invites humankind to follow evil ways. Each person then faces a crucial choice. If they choose to follow the path of evil today, tomorrow they will have no one to blame but themselves. Evil breeds division, weakness, and ultimately defeat.

During times of trauma, and at all times, the Ummah must remain united, for unity is the foundation of strength. Trauma often threatens to tear communities apart, exploiting fear, anger, and grief to sow discord. But survival and healing come through standing together, supporting one another, and resisting the whispers that seek to divide us. Trauma can leave wounds that feel isolating, making it easier for negative forces to pull people apart. Yet, these moments also hold the potential to deepen bonds and foster collective healing. Recognizing the danger of division is the first step toward protecting the Ummah.

Draw a house with many doors. How do you protect your door from any invasion?

126. Be Ready

Chapter 8, Verse 60 (Prepare against them what you ˈbelieversˈ can of ˈmilitaryˈ power and cavalry)

The enemies of Islam do not hesitate to betray it and stab Muslims in the back. In the face of growing hostility, prejudice, and misunderstanding towards Islam today, Muslims must always be prepared to protect themselves.

Trauma from betrayal and attack can leave deep scars, shaking trust and leaving hearts wounded. Yet, readiness is not just about weapons—it is about strengthening faith and community. Preparing ourselves means healing from past wounds, building knowledge, and fostering unity so that we stand strong against both visible and hidden threats. When trauma strikes, feelings of vulnerability and fear can overwhelm us, but readiness rooted in faith and solidarity can transform trauma into strength, allowing us to respond rather than react. Remember, preparation includes nurturing your inner peace and supporting others who carry similar wounds.

Think of three ways you can prepare yourself for the day you may need to defend your faith and community.

127. You Can Do More

Chapter 8, Verse 65 (If there are twenty steadfast among you, they will overcome two hundred. And if there are one hundred of you, they will overcome one thousand of the disbelievers)

This Verse serves as a powerful source of inspiration. Allah reminds us that our true potential is at least ten times greater than what we are currently achieving, and the least we can do is to strive twice as hard.

While self-care is essential for healing trauma, it goes beyond mere rest. It also involves being purposeful and productive in our efforts to rebuild ourselves and our communities. Especially in these challenging times, the affairs of the Ummah call upon us to rise above our pain and work with renewed energy. Trauma can drain our inner resources and cloud our sense of purpose, making it easy to settle for less than what we are capable of, but healing is also about reclaiming our power, rediscovering our strengths, and pushing ourselves gently toward growth, even when it is exhausting.

What are some areas in your life where you feel you have not yet reached your full potential?

128. Unshackle People

Chapter 8, Verse 70 (If Allah finds goodness in your hearts, He will give you better)

There may be only a few prisoners of war you can set free these days, but countless people are held captive by invisible chains of trauma, fear, grief, and oppression. We must always seek ways to ease the burdens of those who suffer, recognizing that trauma often binds people in silence and isolation.

Trauma opens many doors for us to serve, support, and care deeply for those in need, helping to restore their dignity. Trauma can imprison the heart and mind, leaving survivors feeling trapped by memories of pain and feelings of hopelessness. True healing comes when we reach out with empathy and understanding, helping to break those chains, one act of kindness at a time.

What are three ways you can help unshackle people from their burdens?

129. Fight Betrayal

Chapter 9, Verse 12 (But if they break their oaths after making a pledge and attack your faith, then fight the champions of disbelief)

Allah refers to those who betray the trust placed in them as "leaders of disbelief". Being trustworthy means honoring commitments not only to your community and family but also to "strangers" and to yourself.

Trauma often stems from betrayal and broken trust, leaving deep wounds that affect one's ability to trust again. Yet, a true believer strives to uphold promises and protect the trust others place in them, even in the face of hardship. Betrayal can shatter the foundation of relationships and leave survivors feeling vulnerable and isolated. Healing begins with restoring trust, starting with ourselves and extending to others through consistent and sincere acts of compassion.

Think of someone who betrayed you. How did that betrayal affect your heart and your ability to trust? What steps can you take to avoid betraying others?

130. Win Paradise

Chapter 9, Verse 20 (Those who have believed, emigrated, and strived in the cause of Allah with their wealth and their lives are greater in rank in the sight of Allah)

A believer is always striving to race towards the door of Allah, seeking His pleasure above all else. Sacrificing one's wealth, time, and even life for the sake of Allah is a profound way to win that race.

For those who have endured trauma, this race can feel overwhelming or distant, yet it also offers hope and purpose—a path to healing and meaning beyond pain. Trauma can make us feel stuck or lost, as if the finish line is unreachable, but every small step, whether it is seeking forgiveness, helping others, or nurturing one's faith, brings you closer to Allah's mercy and the ultimate victory.

What steps have you taken, or can you take, to win the most important race of your life, pleasing Allah and healing your heart in the process?

131. Victory is a Mindset

Chapter 9, Verse 25 (Indeed Allah has given you ⸢believers⸣ victory on many battlefields)

Victory is not measured by the size of an army on the battlefield, but by the strength of faith in the heart. When we put things into perspective, rely on Allah, and recognize that His door is our only true safety and refuge, only then do we truly deserve His victory.

Looking at the current struggles and suffering of the Ummah, it is easy to feel overwhelmed and question if the Quran's promises still apply to us. Yet, the good news remains that Allah's promise of victory is certain, whether it happens now or later. Trauma can make victory seem impossible or distant, but faith acts as a light in the darkness, reminding us that even in hardship, victory is born in patience. Sometimes, the greatest victories are the quiet, unseen ones within the heart: the acts of healing, hope, and steadfastness amidst trials.

Write a list of prerequisites for victory. Like our mother Khadijah, try to embody the spirit of victory within yourself, even before it fully materializes.

132. Allah's Light

Chapter 9, Verse 32 (But Allah will only allow His light to be perfected)

The enemies of Islam will try, but ultimately fail, to extinguish its light. Allah will always perfect His light, even when we cannot yet see it. With Allah, after every dark night, there is always a bright day.

Trauma can feel like a deep, dark tunnel with no visible way out. It can leave us feeling lost, overwhelmed, and disconnected from hope. But just as Allah's light never fades, we can find that Divine light even in our darkest moments. Seeking that light is one of the most powerful ways to begin healing and emerge from the depths of trauma.

Draw a dark tunnel. When you feel trapped in despair, how can you remind yourself to look for Allah as your ultimate source of light?

133. Deserve Victory

Chapter 9, Verse 38 (What is the matter with you that when you are asked to march forth in the cause of Allah, you cling firmly to ˹your˺ land?)

Allah warns us that if we do not respond when He calls upon us, He is fully capable of replacing us. Victory is easy for Allah. The real question each of us must ask is: Are we contributing to that victory? Does Islam grow stronger or weaker because of our actions?

In times of trauma, it is easy to feel powerless. Yet, healing does not mean inaction, it means finding small, meaningful ways to participate in the collective strength of the Ummah. Your efforts, no matter how small, can be part of a greater victory.

What are three things you are currently doing, or can start doing, to help expedite victory for yourself, your community, and the Ummah?

134. Do Not Be Left Out

Chapter 9, Verse 46 (But Allah disliked that they should go, so He let them lag behind)

Allah reminds us that if we truly intend to bring about victory, we must take all the necessary means. A fight without preparation often leads to defeat. Islam teaches us to do our best and to always be ready for whatever challenges come our way. Unfortunately, as we have witnessed on many occasions, some Muslims refuse to be part of the victory, and some even actively engage in harming and plotting against the Ummah. This betrayal deepens the wounds within our communities and can leave us feeling fragmented. In times of hardship, such divisions only prolong suffering and delay healing. Trauma weakens the bonds that hold communities together, but it also offers a chance to rebuild stronger foundations based on trust, unity, and vigilance. Being prepared is not just about physical safety but also about emotional and spiritual fortitude. Protecting ourselves and the Ummah means safeguarding our hearts from despair and our minds from negativity.

Write a list of precautions you can take to protect your home and the greater house of Islam.

135. Win Either Way

Chapter 9, Verse 52 (Say, "Are you awaiting anything to befall us except one of the two best things: ˹victory or martyrdom˺?")

Nothing will happen to us except what Allah has determined. How comforting it is to hold the certainty that all of our affairs are in the hands of the Most Merciful.

In times of trauma and hardship, this trust becomes a powerful source of peace amid chaos. It reminds us that even in the darkest moments, there is Divine wisdom and mercy beyond our understanding. Those who fight sincerely for Allah's sake will receive one of two blessings: either a victory that fills their hearts with joy or a martyrdom that grants them eternal rest and honor. This truth can provide hope and strength to those suffering, reassuring them that their pain is not in vain and that their endurance has profound meaning. When trauma shakes our world, uncertainty and fear can overwhelm us. Yet, knowing that Allah's decree is just and merciful helps ground our souls. We may not control the outcome, but we can control our actions and intentions.

Think of all the winning options you have when you place your trust in Allah.

136. Enough Support

Chapter 9, Verse 59 (Allah is sufficient for us)

Islam reminds us that we have the strongest support system when we lean on our faith. When people walk away from you in your moments of greatest need, remember that Allah is always in your corner. He is never absent, and never abandoning you.

In times of trauma, feelings of isolation and betrayal can deepen the pain. Yet, turning to the Quran and Sunnah offers a source of comfort, guidance, and unwavering support. They teach us that even when human connections fail, our connection with Allah remains firm. Trauma often shatters trust and leaves wounds that make it hard to rely on others, but faith provides a sanctuary—a safe place to rebuild and find strength. Embodying the teachings of the Quran and Sunnah means nurturing patience, gratitude, and compassion within ourselves, allowing us to heal and rise above the pain.

How can you embody the teachings of the Quran and Sunnah to create a spiritual support system for yourself during difficult times?

137. Man Needs a Tribe

Chapter 9, Verse 71 (The believers, both men and women, are guardians of one another)

Just like victory, healing in Islam is a communal affair. Trauma often isolates individuals, making recovery difficult without connection and support. While professional help is invaluable, it is not always available, accessible, culturally acceptable, or suited to everyone's context. This is why much of the healing in Islam happens when we lean on our personal and communal support networks, grounded in our faith traditions. These networks provide not only practical assistance but also emotional and spiritual comfort, helping trauma survivors regain a sense of safety, belonging, and hope. Healing from trauma is rarely a solo path. It flourishes within a community that fosters trust, understanding, and compassion. Our faith encourages us to create and nurture spaces where people feel safe, seen, heard, and valued beyond their pain.

How can you build a safe and healthy support network around you that embraces sincerity, excellence, and grace?

138. Watch Out

Chapter 9, Verse 75 (And there are some who had made a vow to Allah: "If He gives us from His bounty, we will surely spend in charity and be of the righteous")

People make all kinds of promises, and when Allah grants them what they asked for, many sadly turn their backs on the very source of their blessings. Unfortunately, this betrayal is seen even among some relief workers. When they receive funds or grants meant to aid trauma survivors and refugees, instead of serving those in need, they misuse or keep the resources for themselves. This exploitation deepens the wounds of trauma survivors, who are already vulnerable and in desperate need of support. When those entrusted with care betray that trust, it can shatter survivors' faith in humanity, making healing even more difficult. Trauma survivors depend on honesty, compassion, and integrity from those around them. When these are broken, it compounds their pain and distrust. Recognizing such betrayals is essential in protecting survivors and holding people accountable.

What are some examples of people taking advantage of trauma survivors?

139. Respond

Chapter 9, Verse 83 (You preferred to stay behind the first time, so stay with those ˹helpless˺ who remain behind)

The beloved Prophet forgave and accepted excuses from those who did not join the fighting. Not everyone is physically able or emotionally prepared to engage in battle. Trauma, fear, illness, or other challenges can hold people back. However, we can, and should, still contribute to victory in other meaningful ways by using the blessings and abilities Allah has bestowed upon us. Everyone has a role, whether through prayer, support, counsel, or other forms of service. Trauma can leave people feeling powerless and hesitant to participate. It is important to recognize these barriers without judgment and encourage healing and contribution at one's own pace. Feeling left behind or inadequate can deepen wounds, but understanding and support can help transform those feelings into purposeful action.

What are some reasons people lag behind in contributing to the Ummah? How can you overcome these obstacles?

140. Intention Counts

Chapter 9, Verse 92 (They left with eyes overflowing with tears out of grief that they had nothing to contribute)

There are those who, despite being poor, strive to find a way to spend in the cause of Allah. When no door opens for them to contribute, they walk away with their hearts broken and heavy with grief. This deep yearning to help, paired with helplessness, can be a profound source of emotional pain, fueling survivor guilt, vicarious trauma, and moral injury. Yet, healing begins with the grace of knowing that Allah sees the sincerity in our hearts and rewards our pure intentions, even when our actions seem limited or not enough. Feeling unable to act in the face of overwhelming need can deepen trauma and self-doubt. It is vital to recognize that healing comes from both intention and action, no matter how small. Every sincere effort holds value, and Allah's mercy encompasses the struggles of those who yearn to do good but face barriers.

When you see a need, how can you offer help, no matter how small your role might be?

141. Strive

Chapter 9, Verse 94 (Your deeds will be observed by Allah and His Messenger as well)

It is essential that we do everything to the best of our ability, always striving for the highest standards to please Allah and to emulate the noble Prophets. When we remain mindful of Allah and commit to following the example of the Prophets, even in the midst of hardship and trauma, we nurture hope, not only for ourselves but for the entire Ummah. Imagine how much stronger and more united the Ummah would be if every individual carried this awareness, especially during times of collective pain and suffering.

Trauma can leave us feeling powerless, but striving to uphold faith and noble values amidst adversity is a powerful act of healing. It reminds us that even in brokenness, we can embody strength, patience, and compassion—qualities modeled by the Prophets. This mindful striving can help transform pain into purpose, fostering collective healing.

What three things in your life are truly worth striving for?

142. Trade with Allah

Chapter 9, Verse 111 (Allah has indeed purchased from the believers their lives and wealth in exchange for Paradise)

Allah wants to make a profound deal with the believers. Allah is the buyer, we are the sellers, our souls are the merchandise, and Paradise is the ultimate prize. Dealing with Allah is always a winning transaction.

When trauma strikes, especially the trauma of loss, grief, or deep suffering, we must remember that Allah has taken back what He temporarily loaned us. This awareness can bring comfort and perspective amid heartbreak, reminding us that everything ultimately belongs to Him. Remembering that Allah is in control can bring solace and strength. Our suffering is not unnoticed, and our acts of compassion are deeply valued in His sight. This awareness can help transform pain into purposeful service, creating healing connections even in the darkest of moments.

How can you incorporate the realization that your service to others is a direct deal with Allah more deeply into your daily life?

143. The Source of Ease

Chapter 9, Verse 117 (After the hearts of a group of them had almost faltered)

When every door closes and life feels unbearable, when darkness surrounds you and hope begins to fade, it is in those very moments that the light of ease shines brightest from the Most Merciful.

Trauma often pushes us to the edge, making us question everything and struggle with despair. Yet, Allah's mercy is vast, and His relief can come suddenly, even when we least expect it. Holding onto hope and trusting in the Divine wisdom can be a lifeline during harsh times. During trauma, it is natural to feel overwhelmed and lose faith in relief. But remembering Allah's promise that after hardship comes ease can help anchor the heart.

What are three ways you consciously think well of Allah and trust His mercy during your hardest and darkest moments?

144. When Out of Options

Chapter 9, Verse 118 (They knew there was no refuge from Allah except in Him)

One of the deeds most beloved to Allah and His Prophet is to think well of Allah and have certainty in His promises.

Trauma often shakes our faith and makes us doubt the goodness of life and of Allah's plan. Yet, holding onto hope and trusting in Allah's promises can be a powerful act of healing. It strengthens the soul, restores peace, and helps rebuild broken relationships affected by pain and despair. Hope acts as a protective shield for the soul, especially after trauma. It encourages patience and the ability to envision a future beyond suffering. Conversely, despair can isolate us, deepen our wounds, and strain our connections with others and with Allah.

What are three benefits of maintaining hope during difficult times? How does despair affect your soul and your relationship with others?

145. The Prophet's Heart

Chapter 9, Verse 128 (He is concerned by your suffering, anxious for your well-being)

One of the most beautiful qualities of the beloved Prophet is his tenderness, grace, and deep concern for the Ummah and all of humanity.

In times of trauma and hardship, his compassionate example serves as a source of comfort and hope for those who are hurting. One of the greatest blessings we long for is the pleasure of being among the neighbors of the Prophet in Paradise, a place free from pain and suffering. When trauma overwhelms the heart, remembering the Prophet's mercy and care can help soothe our deep wounds.

Name three things that you believe can bring comfort to the heart of your beloved Prophet.

146. Man's Short Memory

Chapter 10, Verse 21 (When We give people a taste of mercy after being afflicted with a hardship, they swiftly devise plots against Our revelations)

One of the most troubling qualities of human beings is their attitude toward their Lord once the distress has passed. It is common for people to forget the hardships they endured and become ungrateful when ease returns. To protect ourselves from falling into ingratitude, we must learn to appreciate and remember Allah, both in times of ease and in crisis.

After trauma, the mind can struggle with memories of pain, sometimes pushing them away, and sometimes forgetting the lessons learned. This can lead to a fragile relationship with gratitude and faith. Remembering Allah consistently, regardless of life's circumstances, anchors the heart and nurtures healing.

Think of three examples where human memory is short when it comes to fulfilling religious duties.

147. The Ultimate Prize

Chapter 10, Verse 26 (Those who do good will have the finest reward and ˹even˺ more)

For the people of grace, the reward is nothing but Paradise, and even greater than that is the honor of gazing upon the face of their Creator. This promise alone can ignite a deep longing in the hearts of believers, helping them endure and tolerate whatever difficulties they face to attain that ultimate reward.

During times of intense suffering after trauma, the hope of meeting Allah and earning His pleasure becomes a powerful source of comfort. This spiritual vision gives meaning to pain and transforms hardship into a pathway toward healing and eternal success.

What is the ultimate prize for a believer in your understanding? The Quran answers: Allah's pleasure.

148. Some Never Bear Witness

Chapter 10, Verse 35 (Who then is more worthy to be followed: the One Who guides to the truth or those who cannot find the way unless guided?)

A common theme in the Quran is how Allah commands us to bear witness. The problem with humankind is often heedlessness and short memory. Many factors can cause people to remain silent or hesitate to speak out against injustice. Those include fear of retaliation, feelings of powerlessness, trauma-induced numbness, or the pain of reliving wounds by confronting difficult truths. In Islam, we are encouraged to speak up and raise our voices when it is right to do so, while taking care to do so safely whenever possible. Indeed, one of the greatest forms of jihad is to stand firmly against tyranny and oppression by bearing witness to the truth.

Trauma can silence even the strongest voices, making it difficult for survivors and witnesses to speak out. Yet, Islam honors the courage to testify and resist oppression despite fear and pain. Bearing witness becomes an act of healing, empowerment, and safeguarding justice for future generations.

What are some reasons people choose to stay silent in the face of injustice?

149. Neither Fear nor Grief

Chapter 10, Verse 62 (There will certainly be no fear for the close servants of Allah, nor will they grieve)

Those who lean on Allah have no reason to fear or grieve. They find contentment and peace in whatever comes from their Beloved.

Trauma often traps us in painful memories of the past, like depression that keeps us stuck, or in paralyzing fears about the future, as anxiety takes hold. No matter how dark yesterday was, or how uncertain tomorrow may seem, the present moment remains the only reality we truly possess. Learning to live fully in today can be a powerful step toward healing. When trauma weighs heavily on the heart, it can be difficult to let go of past pain or stop worrying about what lies ahead. Yet, Islam teaches us to trust in Allah's plan and find solace in the current moment, where healing begins and life continues. This mindful attitude is an act of faith and surrender to Divine wisdom.

How can you cultivate the ability to live in the present moment, without being overwhelmed by mourning yesterday or fearing tomorrow?

150. Ask for Protection

Chapter 10, Verse 85 (Our Lord! Do not subject us to the persecution of the oppressive people)

This Verse inspires one of the beautiful prayers to protect oneself from participating in oppression.

Trauma, pain, and fear can sometimes cloud our judgment, making it easier to side with injustice, whether out of anger, despair, or survival. But Islam teaches us to guard our hearts and actions, so we do not become instruments of harm to others. Protecting ourselves from taking the side of oppression is not only a moral duty but also a crucial step in healing and preserving our faith. In times of trauma and conflict, emotions can run high, and the risk of contributing to injustice, whether through words, silence, or deeds, can increase. Being mindful of this and seeking Allah's protection through prayer and self-awareness can help us resist the cycles of harm and break free from the grip of trauma.

What are some ways you can protect yourself from siding with injustice?

151. An Ugly Fate

Chapter 10, Verse 92 (Today We will preserve your corpse so that you may become an example for those who come after you)

Allah preserved the body of Pharaoh as a powerful sign, so that we might reflect, take heed, and never forget. It is both terrifying and tragic to witness the arrogance of today's tyrants, repeating the same mistakes with blind pride, as if history did not leave behind a corpse as a warning. Pharaoh challenged Allah until the very end, drowning in the same sea he arrogantly believed he controlled. And yet, even in death, Allah exposed his humiliation to the world. His body, lifeless and bloated, lies as a timeless reminder of Divine justice. And still, in our time, modern-day Pharaohs rise. They oppress, they mock the truth, they claim false power, and just like the Pharaoh of Egypt, they ignore every sign until it is too late. They build empires on the backs of the broken, their hands stained with the blood, sweat, and tears of the innocent. But no one escapes accountability, not in this world, and certainly not in the next.

When you meet Allah, will someone be clutching your neck, demanding justice? Reflect, before you become a lesson.

152. Faith is Safety

Chapter 10, Verse 103 (For it is Our duty to save the believers)

It would have been easy for Allah to guide all of His creation, but His Divine decree is that we strive to find Him. In that struggle, there is wisdom. There is transformation. There is the breaking and the rebuilding. Because when you finally find your Lord, what have you truly lost? This is why healing from trauma is not just about surviving. It is about reclaiming the parts of you that were shattered. It is about tending to your biological, psychological, social, and most importantly, spiritual needs—needs that were often ignored, violated, or denied in the very moments you needed them most. So many walk through life disconnected, from their bodies, from their hearts, and from their Creator, because trauma teaches us to dissociate, to numb, and to forget. But healing means remembering. It means coming back to yourself. And you find yourself only when you find your Lord.

What three acts can help you rediscover who you are?

153. Do Not Get Discouraged

Chapter 11, Verse 12 (Perhaps you ˹O Prophet˺ may wish to give up some of what is revealed to you and may be distressed by it)

People can be negative, cruel, and dismissive. Sometimes their words pierce deeper than wounds you can see. But you get to decide what to do with that. You can absorb it, or you can rise above it, knowing you are not alone in this experience. Even the best of creation, Prophet Muhammad PBUH, was insulted, mocked, and rejected. And yet, Allah reminded him not to grieve, because the role of the Prophet was to deliver the message, not to carry the burden of the rejection. The weight of guidance belongs to Allah alone. Still, let us not minimize the emotional toll of rejection. Being constantly on the receiving end of trauma and being wounded, whether through words, actions, or betrayal, can drain the soul. It can leave you feeling like you are walking through life with open wounds that will never close. But what truly matters is this: you keep walking. You continue the journey of healing, no matter how slow your pace, and no matter how heavy your steps, because every step forward is an act of resistance. Every moment you choose to heal is an act of worship.

What are three tools the Beloved Prophet used to nurse his wounds?

154. No Other Refuge

Chapter 11, Verse 43 (Today no one is protected from Allah's decree except those to whom He shows mercy!)

The son of Prophet Noah believed he could find safety in a towering mountain—A false sense of security in something that looked unshakable, but true protection that day was in the shade of his Lord. People today build emergency kits, map out escape routes, and create backup plans for every possible disaster. And while preparation is wise, we must remember: When calamity strikes, only the Divine plan unfolds. No amount of planning can outmaneuver the decree of Allah. And no amount of running can distance us from what is written.

For those who have endured trauma, this truth can feel terrifying, because control feels like safety, and when you have lived through moments where everything collapsed, it is natural to want guarantees. But healing means learning to surrender without losing your power. It means understanding that your refuge is not in controlling the storm, it is in knowing who shelters you within it.

In your deepest moments of distress, where do you seek refuge?

155. Faith Before Family

Chapter 11, Verse 46 (He is certainly not of your family— he was entirely of unrighteous conduct)

Allah told Prophet Noah that his son was not of his family— Not because of bloodline or biology, but because faith is what truly defines connection in the eyes of Allah. It is a reminder that not all ties are sacred unless they are rooted in belief and righteousness.

For many, trauma does not just hurt individuals. It fractures families. It creates emotional distance, shatters trust, and leaves wounds that echo across generations. Sometimes the people who were meant to protect you were the ones who hurt you most. And sometimes love is present, but safety is not. But trauma does not have to have the final word. One powerful tool for healing is learning how to repair relational ruptures and to mend what was broken, not by erasing the past, but by building new patterns of connection. This can look like openhearted conversations, acts of service, shared spiritual practices, or simply showing up, consistently, gently, and with love.

What are three things that can protect your family in this life and the next?

156. Do Your Part

Chapter 11, Verse 88 (I do not want to do what I am forbidding you from)

The purpose of sending Prophets is to guide their people to the beautiful path they themselves had been guided to—A path of light, truth, and integrity. Their actions never contradicted their words, because they embodied the message before preaching it. This is a reminder for all of us. To claim that we rely on Allah, without doing the inner work, is not enough to change our outer condition. True reliance on Allah is not passive surrender. It is not sitting in silence while hoping for life to get better. It is an active process of showing up, even when you are tired, and even when trauma has convinced you that nothing will ever change. Healing, growth, and transformation require effort. But they also require trust. Trust that if you move toward Allah, even crawling, He will carry you the rest of the way.

For those who carry trauma, this kind of trust can feel terrifying. Because trauma teaches us: "You are alone. You have to do it all yourself". But reliance teaches us: "Do your part, and then rest in the knowledge that Allah never abandons you".

What does true reliance on your Master look like?

157. Fear Only Allah

Chapter 11, Verse 92 (Do you have more regard for my clan than for Allah)

Many nations, driven by fear of social pressure, rejected their noble Prophets. They feared the rejection of society more than the displeasure of their Creator. What a backwards mentality it is to fear the creation and forget the One who created all. But let us not be quick to judge without looking inward. Fear of rejection, humiliation, or abandonment is often rooted in deep pain.

For those who have experienced trauma, especially relational trauma, fitting in can feel like survival. When your nervous system is wired by fear, going against the crowd can feel life threatening, even if it is spiritually right. Still, healing means learning to reclaim your voice, even when it shakes. It means standing in truth, even when you are standing alone, because you know Allah is with you.

Think of three ways to fear the Creator more than what He created.

158. Not in Any Capacity

Chapter 11, Verse 113 (And do not be inclined to the wrongdoers or you will be touched by the Fire)

Allah warns us clearly to not side with injustice. Even remaining silent in the face of oppression can make us complicit. Supporting an oppressor, directly or indirectly, is one of the reasons people are dragged toward Hellfire.

Trauma is not only experienced by the oppressed—it is often perpetuated and prolonged when bystanders watch and stay silent out of fear, comfort, or confusion. And for survivors of trauma, witnessing others defend their oppressor or minimize the pain of oppression can be more damaging than the harm itself. That is why Allah commands us to take a stand. Even if it is hard. Even if it costs us relationships, status, or comfort. Because justice is not optional, it is a Divine responsibility. So whatever you do, make sure you are on the side of justice, not oppression. Even in your home. Even in your silence. Even in your heart.

What three action items can help you stand up for justice and resist injustice?

159. The Power of Storytelling

Chapter 11, Verse 120 (And We relate to you ˹O Prophet˺ the stories of the messengers to reassure your heart)

The stories of the other Prophets served as an anchor for the heart of the beloved Prophet. In moments of sorrow, exhaustion, and rejection, Allah reminded him: "You are not alone". Others before you struggled. Others endured pain, loss, and betrayal, and still, they remained firm in their trust in Allah.

For me personally, one of the most powerful healing tools has been reading and writing about hope in the Quran and Sunnah and reflecting on the timeless stories that show how human beings, no matter how broken they seem or feel, can survive and grow when they place their trust in their Lord. These are not just stories to entertain. They are remedies that heal.

How can storytelling help people heal, especially those carrying trauma?

160. Emotional Availability

Chapter 12, Verse 8 (Surely Joseph and his brother are more beloved to our father)

Prophet Joseph felt safe sharing his distressing dream with his father because Prophet Jacob was emotionally available, attuned, and approachable. He had created a relationship built on trust and a safe space where his son could be vulnerable without fear of judgment or dismissal. This is the kind of emotional presence our children so desperately need and deserve today. Without it, they may carry their fears, confusion, and pain alone, suffering in silence, learning to bury their feelings because no one ever taught them it was safe to speak. But being emotionally available is not something that just happens. It requires intentionality.

Trauma, especially unhealed trauma, can make us emotionally distant. It can pull us into survival mode, making us distracted, irritable, or numb. When we are overwhelmed by our own emotional pain, we may unintentionally miss the emotional needs of those closest to us. That is why healing is not just a personal journey. It is a generational act of mercy.

What does love mean to you? How can you become more emotionally available to your family?

161. Value People

Chapter 12, Verse 20 (They sold him for a cheap price)

The people of the caravan did not realize that the beautiful boy they had just rescued from the well was a noble Prophet. In their rush, they overlooked the immense blessing they held in their hands. Similarly, many times, we take our loved ones for granted, failing to express our love, gratitude, and appreciation until it is too late.

Trauma often teaches us to hold back emotions, to guard our hearts against vulnerability, and sometimes even to disconnect from those closest to us out of fear of loss or pain. But in doing so, we risk losing precious moments that can never be recovered.

Have you ever regretted not expressing love to someone before it was too late? How can you do better next time?

162. Run Away from Evil

Chapter 12, Verse 33 (Joseph prayed, "My Lord! I would rather be in jail than do what they invite me to")

Prophet Joseph faced countless temptations, yet he chose with unwavering strength to resist them all. He decided he would rather be thrown into prison than betray his master's trust or engage in indecency. This teaches us that integrity and faithfulness, even in the face of immense pressure, are greater than any fleeting pleasure or fear of hardship. Remember, private sins and harmful actions, especially those hidden deep in the heart, can block or delay the relief and mercy Allah intends for us. Conversely, private acts of goodness, no matter how small, can accelerate the arrival of victory and healing.

For those carrying trauma, temptation can sometimes feel like a false refuge, an escape from pain, a way to numb or control overwhelming emotions, but these temporary escapes often deepen the wound instead of healing it.

What three temptations do you struggle with? How can you develop the strength to resist them?

163. Ease is a Promise

Chapter 12, Verse 49 (Then after that will come a year in which people will receive abundant rain)

It is a promise from Allah that no matter how long and dark the night may seem, it will always be followed by the light of dawn.

For those enduring protracted trauma, whether from family violence, forced displacement, or the ravages of war, holding onto hope can feel impossible. The darkness can feel endless, the weight unbearable, and the future uncertain. But with Allah, there is always ease after hardship. This is not just a comforting idea, it is a Divine promise, a guarantee from the Most Merciful that relief will come. No matter how deep the wound, how long the struggle, ease will arrive.

Recall a time when ease followed your hardship. How do you keep thinking good about Allah.

164. The Bond of Brotherhood

Chapter 12, Verse 69 (I am indeed your brother! So do not feel distressed)

One of the most beloved deeds to Allah and His Prophet is to check in on others, genuinely ask how they are doing, and to ensure they have what they need. This simple act of care can be a profound source of healing, especially for those carrying hidden wounds and burdens.

Prophet Joseph reassured his brother, saying there was no reason to feel sadness or grief as long as they had each other as siblings. This message highlights the power of connection and mutual support, even amid hardship and loss. Imagine how healthy a community would be if everyone adopted this attitude—checking in, offering support, and standing together through trials. This was the foundation of the Prophetic model in Madinah, a community built on empathy, compassion, and collective healing.

Set aside time, at least once a week, to connect deeply with each of your siblings.

165. Bite on Your Tongue

Chapter 12, Verse 77 (But Joseph suppressed his outrage—revealing nothing to them)

Prophet Joseph treated his siblings with grace and forgiveness, despite all the harm they had caused him. His example teaches us that healing relationships sometimes require patience, compassion, and even the difficult choice to hold back anger.

At times, you might need to bite your tongue and manage your emotions, not to suppress your pain, but to protect what is precious, and to allow space for healing. However, after experiencing trauma, it becomes even more important to respect your own boundaries and preserve your energy. Not every relationship is healthy or worth saving, and it is okay to decide which connections are truly valuable and nurturing.

Reflect: What compromises are you willing to make to save a relationship you value?

166. Complain to Allah

Chapter 12, Verse 86 (I complain of my anguish and sorrow only to Allah)

We should never lose hope in Allah's mercy, no matter how deep the pain or how heavy the heart. Islam honors and allows emotional expression; it does not expect us to hide our grief or pretend we are unaffected.

Prophet Jacob is a profound example of this truth. When he lost sight of his beloved son, he openly complained to Allah, not against Allah, expressing his deep sorrow and anguish. This teaches us that turning to Allah with our pain, honestly and vulnerably, is part of our healing journey.

Reflect on the story of Prophet Jacob as a source of hope.

167. Feeling Desperate is Human

Chapter 12, Verse 110 (And when the messengers despaired)

Even the Prophets, despite their closeness to Allah, have come close to despair. Yet, they found the Divine light—a reminder of Allah's mercy and power, and never doubted the promise of their Lord. Their stories show us that despair is a human experience, but losing hope is a choice we can resist.

One powerful tool that Prophet Joseph used throughout his life was embodying the three qualities of taqwa (mindfulness of Allah), ṣabr (steadfast patience), and iḥsan (grace and excellence in character). No matter what trials and tribulations he faced—betrayal, imprisonment, separation, and many more, he remained rooted in these qualities, which became his anchor through the different tests he endured.

For those carrying trauma, feelings of despair can feel overwhelming and all consuming, but the Prophetic examples teach us that even in the darkest moments, we can choose to lean into faith, patience, and grace toward ourselves and others.

Research and reflect on the stories of three Prophets who came close to despair but never gave up hope.

168. Change Starts With You

Chapter 13, Verse 11 (Allah would never change a people's state ˹of favor˺ until they change their own state ˹of faith˺)

We can change our situation, from bad to good, or from good to bad, based on our actions and intentions. This truth is especially important for trauma survivors, who often feel powerless or trapped by their past wounds. It is crucial to empower them with the reminder that they have agency and the ability to actively participate in healing and transforming their lives.

While external aid and support are valuable, true healing comes from within—from tapping into our inner resources and the organic systems of support we carry in our bodies, minds, hearts, souls, and communities. Healing is not just about fixing what is broken externally; it is about nurturing our inner world, restoring our sense of safety, and reclaiming our strength. We must embody the change we want to see in our lives and in the world. Transformation begins with intentional internal work that ripples outward to affect our environment and relationships.

What are three examples of internal work you can do that could change your external circumstances?

169. Only Good Remains

Chapter 13, Verse 17 (But what benefits people remains on the earth)

Plant now seeds of grace that benefit Allah's creation. Leave behind footprints that make people pray for you, not against you. This includes how you cope with adversity and how you carry your pain and share your story.

Trauma can easily become a cycle, passed down unknowingly from one generation to the next. But imagine the powerful, beautiful memories you could leave for your children if you consciously decide to break the cycle of hurt. Make the firm, healing choice today that "the cycle stops with me".

What legacy are you creating with your words, actions, and your decision to heal?

170. Ultimate Comfort

Chapter 13, Verse 28 (Surely in the remembrance of Allah do hearts find comfort)

One of the deepest joys of a believer is tasting the sweetness of faith and finding comfort in the intimate company of their Lord.

In the midst of life's trials and the wounds trauma leaves behind, this connection can be a profound source of peace and healing. One way to nurture this connection is by spending intentional, heartfelt time with the Book of Allah. Its words have the power to soothe the aching heart, restore hope, and remind us of Allah's mercy and closeness.

What three things bring comfort to your heart?

171. Unwitnessed Victory

Chapter 13, Verse 40 (Whether We show you ˈO Prophetˈ some of what We threaten them with, or cause you to die ˈbefore thatˈ)

When Allah decides a matter, it is His decision alone, and only He has the power to change it.

One struggle many trauma survivors face is the inability to see the end of their story or even to glimpse relief from the painful chapters they are living through. This uncertainty can feel overwhelming, leaving the heart heavy with doubt and despair. Yet, many noble Prophets endured similar trials; some never witnessed the fruits of their labor in this world. Their example teaches us an important truth: we are responsible for the journey, not the destination. Our role is to remain steadfast, to strive with sincerity, and to trust in Allah's wisdom and timing. For those carrying trauma, the waiting can be the hardest part. Feeling that healing or justice may never come can make moving forward seem impossible. But remember, Allah alone dictates the conditions of victory, and His mercy often unfolds in ways beyond our understanding.

Can you accept the possibility that you might never see the fruits of your labor in this life?

172. Unshaken

Chapter 14, Verse 27 (Allah makes the believers steadfast with the firm Word ˹of faith˺ in this worldly life and the Hereafter)

Allah bestows steadfastness upon the believers, both in this life and the next, while He leads tyrants and oppressors astray.

Trauma is heartbreaking and soul aching. It can leave the heart restless, overwhelmed by pain and confusion. For those struggling with trauma, one source of comfort can be the deep conviction and tranquility that comes from knowing this test is temporary, and this life is but a fleeting moment in the vastness of eternity. Holding onto this perspective can help soothe restless hearts and provide strength to endure even the darkest trials.

What are three ways you can nurture and strengthen the faith in your heart?

173. Trust Allah

Chapter 14, Verse 47 (So do not think ˹O Prophet˺ that Allah will fail to keep His promise to His messengers)

Allah made a promise, and He will never break it, that victory ultimately belongs to the believers. It is only a matter of time. Allah is never heedless or unaware when it comes to acts of injustice and oppression. He sees every tear, every cry for help, and every moment of hopelessness experienced by His righteous servants. When they reach the depths of despair, Allah takes charge, and when He is in control, miracles happen—turnarounds beyond human expectation.

For those who have endured trauma and injustice, this truth can be a profound source of hope. Even when the situation feels overwhelming and defeat seems certain, Allah's promise reminds us that no darkness lasts forever, and Divine justice will prevail.

Reflect on the story of the Battle of Hunain.

174. Allah Gives or Holds Back

Chapter 15, Verse 21 (There is not any means ˹of sustenance˺ whose reserves We do not hold)

Everything belongs to Allah, and in His hands are the keys to all that exists within His kingdom. He can open His hands to grant blessings or can hold back according to His Divine wisdom. Whatever He decrees will come to pass, even if we do not understand the reasons in the moment.

It is easy to thank Allah when He gives us what we ask for—comfort, relief, or success. But for those carrying trauma, the hardest test often comes when blessings seem delayed or withheld. During these times, our hearts may feel empty, restless, or overwhelmed by pain, making gratitude feel impossible.

How can you thank Allah when He holds back?

175. Misguidance Breeds Despair

Chapter 15, Verse 56 ("Who would despair of the mercy of their Lord except the misguided?")

Only those who are truly misguided fall into deep despair and give up hope. Giving up on Allah's mercy and justice is never an option, not now, and not ever.

For those carrying trauma, despair can feel like a heavy weight, threatening to extinguish even the smallest spark of hope. But surrendering to hopelessness is itself a form of losing the path. True strength lies in holding tightly to faith, even when the heart is broken and the future uncertain.

What are three things you will never give up on?

176. Keep Going

Chapter 15, Verse 99 (And worship your Lord until the inevitable comes your way)

Worshipping Allah is not a phase, it is a lifelong endeavor.

For those carrying trauma, the journey can feel exhausting, but turning to Allah through sincere worship becomes a source of profound encouragement. In moments of distress, spending intimate, mindful time with Allah, our ultimate refuge and source of comfort, can soothe the deepest wounds.

What are three habits or practices you engage in that can help you draw closer to Allah?

177. Created for Him

Chapter 16, Verse 12 (And He has subjected for your benefit)

A common theme in the Quran is to remind the ungrateful creation of the generosity of their Creator. Though we often fail to show true appreciation for His countless blessings, Allah, in His infinite mercy, multiplies our small good deeds and forgives the sins we commit out of ignorance or arrogance.

For those who are traumatized and emotionally wounded, it can be incredibly difficult to believe that Allah loves them, no matter how disheveled, "damaged", or broken they may feel. But what truly matters is what Allah sees and judges: the sincerity and intentions of the heart. Healing begins when we remember that our worth is not defined by our scars but by our efforts to return to Allah with humility and trust.

How do you show gratitude for the blessings in your life, even when weighed down by hardship?

178. Evil Plots Collapse

Chapter 16, Verse 26 (Indeed, those before them had plotted, but Allah struck at the ˹very˺ foundation of their structure, so the roof collapsed on top of them)

When it comes to the arrogant, those who knowingly deny the truth, they will carry not only their own sins but also the sins of those they misled on their backs on the Day of Judgment. Allah is fully capable of destroying the foundations of all structures built on injustice, oppression, and cruelty.

For those who have experienced trauma, it can be a heavy burden to recognize how cycles of harm and wrongdoing continue to affect us and those around us. Yet accountability and self-reflection are essential steps toward breaking free from these patterns.

Are you carrying a continuous bad deed or harmful pattern with you toward your grave?

179. Different Reception

Chapter 16, Verse 32 (Those whose souls the angels take while they are virtuous)

Allah describes in detail how the angels harshly seize the souls of the wicked and cast them into the Hellfire, while gently taking the blessed souls to the grace of their Lord, into their eternal home of peace and mercy.

For those coping with the trauma of loss and the painful death of loved ones, this profound reality can offer both solace and a call to reflection. Understanding that souls are received differently by their Lord may help us find comfort amid grief, knowing that ultimate peace is reserved for those who lived with faith, patience, and righteousness. It also reminds us that the way we live our lives and nurture our hearts deeply affects the state in which we meet our Lord.

What kind of person will have their soul taken gently by the angels? What steps can you take today, through your actions, intentions, and healing, to help ensure such a peaceful and blessed ending?

180. Forced Migration

Chapter 16, Verse 41 (Those who have migrated in the cause of Allah after being persecuted)

Leaving one's home country is an incredibly painful and disorienting experience. Forcible displacement uproots not only physical safety but also a person's sense of belonging, identity, and security and causes deep wounds that can linger for years.

Allah has promised grace in this life and an even greater reward in the next for those who endure such trials, under one vital condition: perseverance and sincere reliance on Him. This promise offers hope amid the darkness of loss and the layers of uncertainty.

How do you define patience within the current context of mass suffering and forced displacement?

181. Do Not Celebrate Delayed Punishment

Chapter 16, Verse 45 (Do those who devise evil plots feel secure that Allah will not cause the earth to swallow them? Or that the torment will not come upon them in ways they cannot comprehend?)

All the blessings we have come from Allah. It is solely His will to keep them with us or to remove them. When humans challenge their Lord through acts of destruction, corruption, and bloodshed, the punishment from Allah can be sudden and severe, serving as a powerful reminder of Divine justice.

For those who have endured trauma caused by violence and injustice, these realities can be both terrifying and deeply unsettling. Yet, they also remind us of the importance of turning to Allah with sincerity, seeking His mercy and protection.

How can you make your voice recognized by Allah during difficult times?

182. Forbearance

Chapter 16, Verse 61 (If Allah were to punish people 'immediately' for their wrongdoing, He would not have left a single living being on earth)

If Allah treats His creation strictly according to their actions, all of us would be destroyed. Yet, out of His immense mercy, He delays the fate of many, giving space for repentance, redemption, and transformation. At the same time, He has a plan for the arrogant and the oppressors, allowing time for their eventual reckoning.

For those carrying trauma, this Divine patience can be both a source of frustration and hope, a reminder that healing and justice often take time. Allah's delay is not negligence but a merciful opportunity, for growth, for forgiveness, and for eventual accountability.

Can you think of three examples that demonstrate Allah's extraordinary patience?

183. Bring Good

Chapter 16, Verse 76 (Wherever he is sent, he brings no good)

A true believer is like a gentle cloud—quiet, soft, and nourishing, leaving behind only blessings and lasting imprints on hearts. Even in passing, they bring relief, shade, and comfort.

We must strive to be a source of goodness and healing wherever life places us, especially in a world where so many are heavily shackled.

How can you become a safe space for others? Do people feel seen, heard, and held in your presence? When someone is hurting, overwhelmed, or lost, are you the first name they think of?

184. Hold On To Faith

Chapter 16, Verse 106 (Not those who are forced while their hearts are firm in faith)

Allah promises mercy and relief to those who are tested severely yet continue to endure with faith and patience. For every soul burdened by hardship, there is Divine assurance that the pain is not wasted. Every tear, every silent struggle, and every sleepless night is witnessed by Allah.

Reflect on the profound virtue of patience in the story of Prophet Job.

185. Protection through Gratitude

Chapter 16, Verse 112 (so Allah made them taste the clutches of hunger and fear for their misdeeds)

Allah never wrongs His creation. He is Just in all things, even when we struggle to understand the wisdom behind what we experience. When people show sincere gratitude, they protect the blessings they have been given. Gratitude becomes a shield, not only preserving what we have, but also inviting peace and contentment into the heart. But when a people grow arrogant, heedless, or challenge their Lord, the consequences often unfold in ways that affect their collective state—abundance can turn to hardship, and peace to fear. Not as punishment from a cruel Creator, but a wake-up call from the Most Merciful, reminding them to return, reflect, and realign.

For those who have experienced loss or sudden change, these shifts can feel deeply personal and destabilizing. Yet even then, Allah's wisdom is at work, sometimes removing what we cling to in order to redirect us to what is better.

What are three intentional ways you are safeguarding the blessings Allah has entrusted to you?

186. Be a Whole Nation

Chapter 16, Verse 120 (Indeed, Abraham was a model of excellence)

Prophet Abraham was described in the Quran as a nation unto himself, despite being just one man. Why? Because he embodied the strength and moral clarity of an entire people. He stood alone in truth when others followed falsehood. He carried the weight of his community's healing, guidance, and reform on his own shoulders, often in isolation and with great personal sacrifice.

This is especially powerful for those who have felt alone in their values, their pain, or their mission. To be "a nation" does not mean being perfect. It means showing up with integrity, even when you are depleted. It means holding on to faith when others let go. It means choosing healing, justice, and mercy, especially when it costs you.

Reflect on why Prophet Abraham was honored with such a title.

187. Center Palestine

Chapter 17, Verse 1 (From the Sacred Mosque to the Farthest Mosque whose surroundings We have blessed)

Throughout the Quran, Allah speaks of the sacredness and blessings of the Holy Land, offering not only spiritual guidance, but also remedies for the deep wounds tied to it. For many, Palestine is not just a geographic location; it is a symbol of both faith and generational pain. It carries both the beauty of revelation and the burden of injustice. We must teach our children that Palestine is the beating heart of the Ummah, not just because of its historical and religious significance, but because it represents our collective memory, our struggle for justice, and our responsibility to uphold the dignity of all who are oppressed. When children understand the spiritual, emotional, and human importance of our sacred places, they grow up connected, not just politically, but compassionately. They learn that to care is an act of worship, and that silence in the face of suffering is never neutral.

Take time to research how Palestine and its sacred sites are mentioned in the Quran and Sunnah. Then, gather as a family to reflect.

188. Victory Starts With You

Chapter 17, Verse 8 (But if you return ˹to sin˺, We will return ˹to punishment˺)

Victory—true, lasting victory, comes when we change ourselves. It begins when we return sincerely to the teachings of our religion, especially in moments of confusion, loss, and despair. Healing our collective condition starts with individual alignment: hearts purified, priorities reset, and actions rooted in sincerity. If each of us were to set our priorities straight, returning to justice, compassion, humility, and accountability, the state of the Ummah would transform. But this change does not happen overnight. It often begins in the quiet, private struggles: the grief we carry alone, the pain we do not talk about, and the disconnection we feel even while trying to hold on to faith.

Reflect on the story of the Battle of Uhud.

189. Work for the Hereafter

Chapter 17, Verse 19 (But whoever desires the Hereafter and strives for it accordingly, and is a ˹true˺ believer, it is they whose striving will be appreciated)

Some people chase the fleeting pleasures of this world, and they will receive only what Allah has already written for them. No more, no less. Others anchor their hearts in the hereafter, enduring hardship and sacrificing ease, and for them, Allah has promised a reward that no eye has seen and no heart can fully imagine.

For those who have experienced trauma, loss, or injustice, the hereafter is not just a hope—it is a reassurance that what was broken here will be repaired there. That what was taken from you unjustly will be returned in full. That every unseen act of patience, every silent tear, every ounce of dignity you held onto when it was hard, will be rewarded.

How do you put things into perspective when comparing this life to the next?

190. Do Not Exceed in Revenge

Chapter 17, Verse 33 (But do not let them exceed limits in retaliation)

Allah has promised His support to those who are oppressed. His justice is not delayed, even when it feels like the world has turned a blind eye. He hears the silent cries, sees the hidden wounds, and never forgets the pain of the victim. But when victory comes, and it will, by His permission, those who were once victims must be careful not to become the very thing they suffered from. Power is a test. And trauma, if left unhealed, can twist into vengeance, bitterness, and cycles of harm. Islam does not deny the right to seek justice, but it sets Divine boundaries to ensure that justice does not turn into cruelty.

What are three ways people exceed Allah's boundaries when retaliating against the source of their trauma? How can you avoid that?

191. Mind the Signs

Chapter 17, Verse 59 (We only send the signs as a warning)

When Satan challenged his Lord, vowing to mislead all the children of Adam, Allah responded with authority and assurance: "You may try, but you will never have power over My true servants—those who place their trust in Me and seek refuge in Me". This Divine promise is a reminder: no matter how heavy the whispers, the temptations, or the pain we carry, those who sincerely lean on Allah, even while struggling, are protected in ways they may not even realize.

In times of trauma, confusion, or loss, it can feel like darkness is closing in. But Allah continues to send both subtle (covert) and clear (overt) signs through the events around us, reminding us to pause, reflect, and return. Nothing in this world happens without wisdom, even if that wisdom is hidden from us in the moment. Human beings are not meant to carry life's burdens alone. We are meant to tune in and to surrender.

Reflect on the story of the three men trapped in a cave, as told by the Prophet (PBUH).

192. Man, the Best of Creation

Chapter 17, Verse 70 (Indeed, We have dignified the children of Adam)

Allah has honored the children of Adam and elevated them above all of His creation. This Divine honor is not just a status, it is a trust. With privilege comes responsibility: the duty to care, to heal, to build, and to leave the world better than we found it.

In a world filled with injustice, pain, and human-caused suffering, this trust becomes even more sacred. We are not merely observers of hardship. We are called to be agents of healing, even when we ourselves are hurting. For those who carry trauma, this truth is both a comfort and a challenge. You are not defined by what you have endured, but by how you choose to respond, rise, and reflect Allah's mercy in your actions.

What three qualities make man the best of creation?

193. Truth Prevails

Chapter 17, Verse 81 ("The truth has come and falsehood has vanished. Indeed, falsehood is bound to vanish")

Allah has promised that no matter how long the dark era of falsehood and injustice may seem to last, the light of truth will inevitably overcome it. This Divine assurance is a beacon of hope for those trapped in despair, pain, and oppression, reminding us that no matter how heavy the darkness feels, it is never permanent.

For those who have endured the trauma of betrayal or injustice, this promise is both a source of solace and a test of patience. It can be incredibly hard to hold onto certainty when the world around you seems overwhelmed by lies and cruelty. Yet, the reality of this promise means that every hardship, every tear, every suppressed voice, and every act of resistance is part of a greater unfolding.

How do you maintain certainty that truth will eventually prevail, especially when the pain feels endless? How can you be a bearer of that light in your own sphere, no matter how small?

194. Compete Only with Yourself

Chapter 18, Verse 24 (Say, "I trust my Lord will guide me to what is more right than this")

Always ask Allah to make you better every day and in every aspect of your life, especially in matters of faith and spirituality.

Healing is a journey, not a destination, and growth often comes through small, steady steps rather than big sudden leaps. When it comes to trauma, this is especially important. Even on the hardest days, committing to progress, no matter how small, honors the process of healing. It means showing up for yourself with patience, kindness, and faith, even when the wounds feel raw and the path feels uncertain.

At the end of each day, reflect deeply: How can you be better than you were yesterday—in your heart, your actions, and your relationship with Allah and His creation?

195. Everything is Recorded

Chapter 18, Verse 49 (What kind of record is this that does not leave any sin, small or large, unlisted?)

To realize that nothing is hidden from Allah can bring profound comfort to those who have suffered injustice. Every hardship is seen and known by the Most Merciful. No act of oppression goes unnoticed, and no transgression escapes His justice. At the same time, this awareness calls us to examine our own actions carefully. Are we taking precautions to ensure that acts of oppression or injustice, whether in word, deed, or neglect, do not find their way into our own book of deeds?

For those carrying trauma, this reflection can be especially powerful. It reminds us that healing begins not only by seeking justice externally, but also by nurturing justice within ourselves, by refusing to perpetuate cycles of harm, even when hurt runs deep.

Ask yourself: How am I guarding my heart and actions against becoming a source of pain or injustice to others?

196. Some Deeds Weigh Nothing

Chapter 18, Verse 105 (Rendering their deeds void, so We will not give their deeds any weight on Judgment Day)

Some of Allah's creation will arrive on the Day of Judgment carrying mountains of good deeds, yet they will still enter the Hellfire. This happens because they performed good deeds publicly but engaged in wrongdoing privately, and because their actions were tainted by crooked motives and insincere intentions.

For those responding to trauma, whether as relief workers, caregivers, or supporters, this is a vital reminder to continually examine their intentions. True healing and support come only when actions are done sincerely for Allah's sake, free from pride, seeking recognition, or personal gain. The sincerity behind our efforts can make all the difference, not just in how others receive our help, but in how Allah accepts it.

Think of three things you have done or said that others praised or admired. What was your true motive behind those acts?

197. Speak with Allah

Chapter 19, Verse 3 (When he cried out to his Lord privately)

We all need to approach our Lord with humility, respect, and awe. Yet, as human beings, we are often hasty; we want things immediately, craving instant relief and answers. In our impatience, many times we fail to show Allah the honor and reverence He truly deserves.

For trauma survivors, this impatience can be especially challenging. When the heart is wounded and the soul is restless, it is easy to feel distant from Allah or to rush prayers and supplications, hoping for quick relief. But true connection requires presence, patience, and deep respect.

Reflect on the sacredness of speaking with Allah. What are three essential etiquettes we should observe when communicating with Him?

198. Coping with Death Wishes

Chapter 19, Verse 23 (She cried, "Alas! I wish I had died before this, and was a thing long forgotten!")

Allah has given us permission to express our emotions openly and to complain and pour out our hearts to Him, but never to blame or question His wisdom unjustly. This sacred space of turning to Allah with our pain is a vital part of healing. Human beings need to process their feelings, especially after trauma or deep suffering, but it is essential to do so in ways that are halal, safe, and healthy, through prayer, seeking support and constructive outlets that nurture the soul rather than harm it. The Quran addresses the topic of suicide with great seriousness, emphasizing the sanctity of life and reminding us that despair is a test, not an end. Suicide is forbidden because it cuts short the opportunity for healing and the chance for Allah's mercy to reach us. This message is both a warning and a hope, that even when the darkness feels overwhelming, relief can come, and life can be restored.

How does the Quran's guidance on suicide shape your understanding of the topic? What halal, safe, and healthy ways can you adopt to process difficult emotions instead of resorting to self-harm?

199. Be a Source of Blessings

Chapter 19, Verse 31 (He has made me a blessing wherever I go)

One of the most beautiful acts of worship that draws us closer to Allah is showing kindness to our parents, especially our mothers, who often carry unseen burdens and sacrifices. Alongside this, blessing others through gentle and gracious conduct, even when kindness is directed towards total strangers, spreads healing in a world that so often feels uncaring.

For those who have experienced trauma or hardship, acts of kindness are not just good deeds; they are powerful steps toward restoring trust, building connection, and breaking cycles of pain. Kindness can be a balm for the wounded hearts, both for the giver and the receiver.

What have you gifted your loved ones, or even a complete stranger, today?

200. Meeting Allah

Chapter 19, Verse 95 (And each of them will return to Him on the Day of Judgment all alone)

Every single one of Allah's creation will stand before their Lord alone. No one else will carry their deeds or speak on their behalf. This inevitable meeting is both a solemn reality and a moment of profound significance. We must prepare ourselves for that encounter, not just in outward acts, but also with sincere hearts shaped by mercy, kindness, and grace. Filling our book of deeds with compassionate actions and gentle mercy is one of the best ways to ready ourselves for that day.

For those who have experienced trauma, this preparation can carry even deeper meaning. Trauma can leave us feeling isolated and broken, but the promise of standing before Allah alone reminds us that our struggles and our healing journey are seen intimately by the One who knows us best.

What are your thoughts, feelings, and behaviors when you contemplate the idea of meeting Allah?

201. Facing Tyranny

Chapter 20, Verse 24 (Go to Pharaoh, for he has truly transgressed 'all bounds')

When Allah commanded Prophet Moses to confront the Pharaoh, he sought both Divine support from his Lord and practical, worldly support from his brother, Prophet Aaron. This balance of spiritual reliance and human connection was essential for facing overwhelming tyranny and injustice.

For those who endure trauma and oppression, having a support network, both spiritual and human, is vital. The journey through pain and struggle can feel isolating, but just as Prophet Moses did not face his trials alone, neither should we.

Who makes up your support network when you face injustice or hardship?

202. Prophet Moses

Chapter 20, Verse 41 (And I have selected you for My service)

Prophet Moses grew up under the direct supervision of his Lord, within the house of his enemy. He was strong and trustworthy—qualities that earned him Allah's continual support throughout his trials. His story teaches us about faith and patience in the face of oppression and trauma.

For those who have faced similar difficulties, Prophet Moses' journey is a powerful reminder that strength can grow even in the harshest environments, and that perseverance paired with trust in Allah brings Divine support.

What are three qualities of Prophet Moses that you admire most?

203. Find Good in "Bad"

Chapter 20, Verse 73 (So He may forgive our sins)

When the Pharaoh threatened the magicians who defied him and chose to follow Prophet Moses, the punishment they faced was, in reality, a form of cleansing—a test that led to their ultimate salvation and freedom. Sometimes, what we instinctively try to run away from is actually the very source of our liberation and growth.

For those carrying wounds, this truth can be difficult to grasp. Painful experiences often feel overwhelming and unbearable, yet within them may lie the seeds of healing and transformation, if we can find the courage to face and understand them.

Look at the aspects of your life that seem to be falling apart or causing you distress. How can you begin to see any good emerging from these challenges?

204. Hasten Towards Allah

Chapter 20, Verse 84 (And I have hastened to You, my Lord, so You will be pleased)

Allah presents His creation with countless opportunities to serve Him and fulfill their purpose. Like Prophet Moses, who hastened towards his Lord out of deep obedience and love, we too are called to respond swiftly and sincerely to Allah's commands.

For those who have experienced trauma, responding to Allah's guidance can be both a source of healing and a challenge. Trauma often brings feelings of hesitation, doubt, or fatigue, making it hard to move forward. Yet, just as Moses moved with urgency and trust despite the overwhelming trials around him, we are encouraged to approach our Lord with a heart full of resolve and hope.

What is your speed and attitude when it comes to obeying Allah's orders?

205. A Heavy Burden

Chapter 20, Verse 111 (And all faces will be humbled before the Ever-Living, All-Sustaining. And those burdened with wrongdoing will be in loss)

One of the heaviest burdens anyone will carry on the Day of Judgment is the weight of violating the rights of others. Such transgressions leave deep wounds, not only in this life but also in the hereafter. It is said that it is better to be the son of Adam who dies by murder than to be the son of Adam who commits the murder, for the oppressor bears a heavy load when they meet Allah.

For those who have experienced trauma, especially from injustice or abuse, this reminder underscores the serious consequences of harming others. Healing begins not only with seeking justice but also with holding ourselves accountable, ensuring we do not end up perpetuating harm.

What deeds are you preparing to present to your Lord?

206. Allah's Kingdom

Chapter 21, Verse 23 (He cannot be questioned about what He does, but they will ˹all˺ be questioned)

The truth will have the final word over falsehood. It is only a matter of time before this Divine promise becomes reality. In the face of uncertainty and chaos, we must align our actions with Allah's plan, trusting His infinite wisdom even when doubt clouds our hearts.

For those who have endured trauma, pain and confusion may tempt us to question or lose faith, but remembering that truth ultimately prevails helps anchor us.

In these turbulent times, how can you ensure that you remain a vital piece in the Divine plan?

207. The Test of Comfort

Chapter 21, Verse 35 (And We test you ˹O humanity˺ with good and evil as a trial)

Allah tests us, not only through hardships and difficulties, but also through ease and comfort.

Those who fight on the frontlines may face a relatively clearer test, as their choices often come down to victory or martyrdom. However, for many, the test of comfort is far more complex and challenging: to bear witness to the trauma, violence, and violation of the sacred while feeling helpless to intervene. This kind of test, enduring pain from a distance, watching suffering unfold, and struggling with feelings of powerlessness, can weigh heavily on the heart and spirit causing vicarious trauma, survivor guilt, and moral injury. It challenges our faith in profound ways.

What three things might be your personal test in this life?

208. Do Not Throw Temper Tantrum

Chapter 21, Verse 37 (Humankind is made of haste)

Man is created hasty. We want things, and we want them now. When our desires are not fulfilled right away, we sometimes respond with a spiritual temper tantrum, expressing frustration or doubt toward our Creator. Yet, this impatience is not the way a slave should behave when interacting with his Master.

In the context of trauma, this hasty reaction can be even more intense. Pain and suffering often amplify our desire for quick relief and answers, making the test of patience even harder. However, true patience means that our steadfastness and trust in Allah must begin right at the moment of crisis, when the initial pain or hardship strikes.

What does "patience is at the first shock" mean to you?

209. Nothing Overwhelms Allah

Chapter 21, Verse 69 (We ordered, "O fire! Be cool and safe for Abraham!")

When you are truly with Allah, even a blazing fire becomes a place of coolness and peace. Nothing can overwhelm or defeat the power of Allah's protection.

For those who have experienced trauma, this truth offers profound comfort: no matter how fierce the trials or how intense the suffering, Allah's presence can transform even the most painful moments into spaces of calm and healing.

Study the story of Prophet Abraham when thrown into the fire by his people for his unwavering faith.

210. The Power of Prayer

Chapter 21, Verse 76 (We responded to him)

When Prophet Noah sincerely called upon his Lord, Allah caused the flood that drowned a corrupt humanity, cleansing the earth of injustice. A similar response was granted to other Prophets who earnestly prayed for relief and justice in the face of overwhelming trials.

For those who endure trauma, this reminds us never to underestimate the power of sincere supplication. Prayer is not just a plea; it is a profound connection to Allah's mercy and a source of strength, even when the world seems to be falling apart.

When you raise your hands in prayer, are you confident that Allah will answer you?

211. Only Allah Heals Wounds

Chapter 21, Verse 83 ("I have been touched with adversity, and You are the Most Merciful of the merciful")

Allah responds to all who call upon Him, not only the Prophets. When Allah takes charge of the healing process, He is able to mend all wounds, no matter how deep or infected they may be.

For those who carry trauma—emotional, physical, or spiritual, this Divine healing offers profound hope. Even the deepest scars can be transformed through Allah's mercy and care. Trusting Him in our moments of need opens the door to restoration that no human help alone can ever provide.

Whom do you turn to when you are in need and when your heart feels heavy?

212. Inherit the Land

Chapter 21, Verse 105 (We decreed in the Scriptures: "My righteous servants shall inherit the land")

In times of hardship, one might begin to question the Divine promise that the believers will ultimately achieve victory and be entrusted with the stewardship and healing of the world. Such doubts can weigh heavily on a wounded heart, especially when suffering seems endless and justice delayed. Having firm faith is a powerful way to dispel these doubts and bring peace to the soul. Faith acts as a healing balm, restoring trust in Allah's wisdom and timing, even when the pain feels overwhelming.

How can you cleanse your heart of doubts about your Creator in moments of uncertainty?

213. Do Not Worship Conditionally

Chapter 22, Verse 11 (And there are some who worship Allah on the verge ⸢of faith⸣)

There are those who worship Allah on the edge—meaning their faith is conditional and transactional. Their relationship with their Lord is based on expecting rewards or fearing punishment, rather than genuine love and devotion. In contrast, the true servants of Allah are transformed through sincere love, trust, and a deep commitment to serving Him, regardless of life's circumstances.

For those who have experienced trauma, it can be tempting to approach faith as a kind of transaction: "If I am patient or obedient, I should be spared pain". Yet true healing and spiritual growth come from embracing a relationship with Allah that is unconditional, rooted in love and trust even amidst suffering.

How can you ensure that your relationship with Allah is not transactional but born from genuine love and submission?

214. No Honor for the Disgraced

Chapter 22, Verse 18 (And whoever Allah disgraces, none can honor)

Whomever Allah chooses to disgrace, no one else can grant them true honor. When the path toward Allah is filled with difficulties and trials, many may stumble and fall away from the straight path, losing grace.

For trauma survivors, the struggle to maintain faith and honor amid pain can feel overwhelming. It is during these difficult moments that the risk of despair, harmful choices, or losing one's moral compass is greatest. But remembering that true honor comes only from Allah helps anchor the heart, encouraging mindful acts that align with our high values.

Write a list of actions and behaviors that lead to disgrace—those that harm your soul, your faith, or your relationships with others. How can you protect yourself from disgrace?

215. Allah Defends the Oppressed

Chapter 22, Verse 38 (Indeed, Allah defends those who believe)

Allah has made a promise, and Allah never breaks His promise, that He Himself will defend the oppressed. This Divine protection and justice may come in many different forms, some of which we may not immediately recognize or understand. Allah defends His servants in ways that transcend human comprehension, with wisdom that often unfolds over time.

For those who have witnessed or experienced trauma, it can be deeply painful to wait for justice or healing. When suffering continues, it is natural to feel confused, even disheartened. But part of our spiritual grounding lies in trusting that Allah's might and mercy are always at work, even when we cannot see the full picture.

How can you still witness Allah's power and justice in a world full of oppression and suffering?

216. Islam Allows Self-defense

Chapter 22, Verse 39 (Permission ˹to fight back˺ is ˹hereby˺ granted to those being fought, for they have been wronged)

The oppressed and those who have been forcibly displaced from their homes have both the right and the permission from Allah to defend themselves. Self-defense is not only a human right, but also a deeply spiritual act of preserving life, dignity, and justice. In today's world, we witness glaring double standards. When Muslims stand up and fight back in defense of their lives, lands, and rights, they are often labeled "terrorists" or "barbaric". These words are meant to dehumanize and demoralize. But this is not new. Even the best of creation, our beloved Prophet, and his companions were mocked, demonized, and persecuted for defending the truth. Yet, they stood their ground with faith, dignity, and restraint.

For survivors of trauma, especially those who come from or live in communities under siege, whether by war, occupation, racism, or systemic injustice, self-defense can be physical, emotional, spiritual, or all of the above.

How do you practice self-defense as an individual, a family, and a community?

217. The Best Supporter

Chapter 22, Verse 78 (Hold fast to Allah. He ˈaloneˈ is your Guardian. What an excellent Guardian, and what an excellent Helper!)

If we could just hold tightly to the rope of Allah, we would be leaning on the strongest and most unshakable support. But we often forget, because we are human, and because life, pain, and trauma can cloud our hearts and distract our souls. We forget that Allah is the One in ultimate control. In our desperation, we sometimes seek help from everyone and everything except Him. We may turn to people, systems, or temporary distractions, hoping they will carry our burdens, but true healing comes only from being connected to Allah.

For those who have experienced deep trauma, this forgetfulness is not always intentional. It could be a survival mechanism. Reconnecting with Allah, gently and slowly, can restore a sense of grounding, calm, and spiritual safety.

What does it mean for you to be "with Allah"? Do you feel His presence in your life?

218. Build, Do Not Destroy

Chapter 23, Verse 71 (Had the truth followed their desires, the heavens, the earth, and all those in them would have certainly been corrupted)

It is a mercy that Allah has ultimate control over the universe. If human beings were left to follow their every desire without limits, the world would be overwhelmed with corruption, injustice, and destruction. In a world where trauma, violence, and oppression are often inflicted by those in power, we are reminded that unchecked human desire, especially when driven by ego, greed, or vengeance, can destroy lives and communities. This is why Divine boundaries and guidance are not burdens, but safeguards. They are protections for the soul of the individual and that of the society. Believers are not meant to be passive observers. We are called to take part in healing and rebuilding, not in injuring, breaking, or tearing people down. Whether through words, actions, or silence, we are either contributing to the healing of our world or adding to its pain.

What is your personal definition of corruption? In your thoughts, behaviors, or choices, how do you protect yourself from falling into patterns that harm yourself or others?

219. Take Refuge from Injustice

Chapter 23, Verse 94 (My Lord, do not count me among the wrongdoing people)

One thing we must avoid at all costs is being part of harming others, physically, emotionally, socially, spiritually, or in any other way. Causing harm to Allah's creation, whether intentionally or carelessly, carries heavy consequences in this life and the next. When you are tempted by anger, pain, peer pressure, or unhealed wounds to take part in hurting someone else, pause. Remember the words of Allah, and recite a prayer for protection against your lower self.

Often, those who harm others are themselves carrying unresolved trauma. But passing that pain forward only deepens the cycle. What happened to you can explain, but cannot excuse, your choices. Choosing not to harm others is a powerful act of healing, for them, and for you.

What are some ways you are actively resisting the urge to harm others? How do you respond when your own trauma or pain tempts you to lash out?

220. Work Hard Till the End

Chapter 23, Verse 118 (And say (O Prophet) "My Lord, forgive and have mercy, for you are the best of those who show mercy")

Allah creates nothing haphazardly. Everything He brings into existence has purpose, order, and wisdom, including you. He created us not just to worship Him, but also to take care of His creation with compassion, justice, and responsibility, until we return to Him.

But in a world filled with trauma, injustice, and emotional exhaustion, it is easy to burn out, especially when you carry the pain of others or your own unhealed wounds. Many people pour themselves into doing good, only to find themselves depleted, resentful, or disconnected from the very purpose that once fueled them. Islam teaches us balance. Even the Prophet, while tirelessly serving others, would retreat for rest, reflection, and connection with Allah. We are not meant to be endlessly productive. We are meant to be intentionally present.

How can you engage in good deeds daily without losing your spiritual energy?

221. Do Not Spread Rumors

Chapter 24, Verse 15 (When you passed it from one tongue to the other)

When our mother Aisha (may Allah be pleased with her) was wrongly accused and slandered, she turned to Allah with full trust and reliance. In response, Allah revealed Verses from the Quran to clear her name and restore her honor. This story is not just about vindication, it is about the deep, intimate relationship between Allah and the believers, especially those who are wronged.

When no one else fully understands your pain… when even your character is under attack… when the wound is invisible but overwhelming…Allah sees. Allah knows. And Allah responds, in His perfect timing. For survivors of slander, abuse, or betrayal, the story of Aisha is a profound reminder: being harmed unjustly does not reduce your worth in the sight of Allah. If anything, your patience, dignity, and trust in Him can elevate your status.

What emotions come up when you think about the story of Aisha, the mother of the believers, and what she endured?

222. Joy is Sunnah

Chapter 24, Verse 32 (Marry off the ˹free˺ singles among you, as well as the righteous of your bondmen and bondwomen)

Joy is a part of Islam, even in the midst of pain, hardship, or uncertainty. No matter how dark or distressing the situation of the Ummah became, the beloved Prophet never canceled Eid or other moments of collective joy. He taught us that joy is not a denial of pain, but a necessary act of gratitude and spiritual grounding. Yes, we grieve for the oppressed. We mourn our losses. We carry the weight of trauma, both personal and communal. But Islam teaches us that holding space for grief does not mean we must erase celebration. Remembering the blessings, cherishing moments of togetherness, and finding light amid the darkness are all part of healing. Joy, especially during difficult times, becomes an act of resistance.

What are three meaningful ways you can still celebrate despite these dark days for the Ummah?

223. Submission Equals Success

Chapter 24, Verse 51 (To say, "We hear and obey". It is they who will ˹truly˺ succeed)

The true believers, when invited to respond to Allah and His Messenger, do not hesitate. They listen and obey. That sincere submission is their path to success, both in this life and the next. But let us be honest: submission to the Divine will is not always easy. It can feel confusing, overwhelming, even heartbreaking, especially when what Allah decrees appears to contradict our desires, comfort, or understanding. It takes someone deeply trusting to be truly pleased with whatever Allah decides. This is not just about obedience; it is about faith rooted in love and unwavering certainty in the wisdom of the Creator.

For trauma survivors, painful tests are not punishments. They are invitations to draw nearer to Allah, to surrender without losing ourselves, and to trust that Divine mercy is always at work, even when we do not immediately see it.

What emotions arise when you think about the story of Prophet Ishmael and the command to be sacrificed? Have you ever faced a test where surrendering to Allah felt almost impossible?

224. Turning Fear into Safety

Chapter 24, Verse 55 (And will indeed change their fear into security)

Those who believe and do good, will, by Allah's promise, inherit the earth. They will be empowered, and their state of fear will be transformed into safety and peace. This is not just a reward in the afterlife; it is a promise of dignity and restoration even in this world.

Now imagine how this Divine promise can offer deep comfort to those shackled by the chains of trauma like people who have lived under occupation, abuse, war, oppression, or fear. For someone who has lost their sense of safety or agency, these words are not just hopeful; they are healing. They affirm that your current state of pain is not permanent, and that Allah sees your endurance, your belief, and your righteous actions.

How does faith earn you inheritance, empowerment, and safety from fear?

225. Do Not Abandon the Quran

Chapter 25, Verse 30 (The Messenger has cried, "O my Lord! My people have indeed received this Quran with neglect")

This Verse, which we should deeply reflect upon, reveals that the beloved Prophet expressed to Allah his sorrow that many of his people had abandoned the Quran. This abandonment is not just a neglect of words, but a distancing from a source of guidance, healing, and spiritual nourishment. One profound way to honor the Prophet is to approach both his Sunnah and the words of Allah with genuine awe, respect, and sincerity. The Quran is more than scripture—it is a living light that can soothe wounded hearts, guide lost souls, and rebuild shattered lives.

When trauma and hardship cloud our vision, turning back to the Quran can be an act of reclaiming hope and connection with our Creator. In times of pain and confusion, it is easy to drift away from this vital source of comfort. But to abandon the Quran is to lose the most vital anchor for a believer.

How can you ensure that you do not abandon the Quran, especially when life feels overwhelming or when your heart is heavy?

225

226. Do Not Worship Yourself

Chapter 25, Verse 43 (Have you seen 'O Prophet' the one who has taken their own desires as their god?)

Many people unknowingly make their desires their gods when they place their lust for this life, personal interests, and agendas above the word of Allah. This form of self-worship can be subtle but destructive as it can shift the heart away from its true purpose and traps the soul in endless dissatisfaction. One important way to avoid worshipping ourselves is to cultivate flexibility and open-mindedness, especially in how we approach healing and growth.

Trauma teaches us that healing is rarely linear and that no single path fits everyone. Clinging rigidly to our own desires or preconceived ideas can block the mercy and guidance Allah wants to send our way. True submission requires humility and acknowledging that our will is limited and that Allah's plan is greater. When we elevate our own desires above Allah's word, we risk deepening spiritual wounds and losing sight of the power of healing that comes from surrender.

In what ways might people worship themselves without realizing it? What steps can you take to ensure your desires align with Allah's guidance?

227. Pay Attention

Chapter 25, Verse 50 (We certainly disperse it among them so they may be mindful, but most people persist in ungratefulness)

Most of Allah's servants have eyes, ears, hearts, and minds, yet many do not use these precious faculties to draw closer to Him. Instead, they misuse Allah's blessings by turning away from His guidance and disobeying His commands. This spiritual neglect can be a form of deep self-harm, cutting ourselves off from our very source of healing.

For those carrying trauma, this disconnect can feel like being trapped in darkness, even when the light is all around. Sometimes pain and fear make it difficult to recognize or accept the truth. But Allah's mercy is constant, inviting us to return and heal.

List three ways people turn their backs on the truth. What steps can you take to pay attention and open your eyes, ears, heart, and mind toward Allah's guidance and mercy?

228. Hold Firmly

Chapter 25, Verse 77 (Say, ˹O Prophet,˺ "You ˹all˺ would not ˹even˺ matter to my Lord were it not for your faith ˹in Him˺")

Allah's attention and care for His creation are deeply connected to their calling upon Him. If not for their sincere supplications, His mercy and intervention would not manifest in their lives. Never underestimate the power of your prayer. Your heartfelt supplication is a lifeline, a refuge, and a source of profound healing.

In the midst of trauma and hardship, supplication becomes more than just words; it is the believer's most powerful weapon. It opens the doors to Divine mercy, provides comfort to the broken heart, and strengthens the spirit when everything else feels fragile. Pray for yourself, for your loved ones, for the Ummah, and for all humanity, because healing and relief come through turning to Allah with trust and sincerity.

What are your three top go-to tools for healing? Is supplication one of them?

229. A Fatal Flaw

Chapter 26, Verse 19 (Then you did what you did, being ˹utterly˺ ungrateful!)

The arrogant seldom admit their faults, if they admit them at all. The Pharaoh of Egypt, after deliberately murdering thousands, had the audacity to accuse Prophet Moses of killing one man by mistake. This same arrogance is painfully evident in many of today's tyrants and oppressors, who refuse to acknowledge the harm they cause.

For survivors of injustice, this refusal to admit wrongdoing can deepen wounds and prolong suffering. Healing often feels impossible when there is no accountability or acknowledgment of the pain inflicted. The absence of an apology or justice can leave scars that are difficult to overcome.

Can true healing happen without receiving an apology or acknowledgment of harm?

230. Be with Allah

**Chapter 26, Verse 62 (Moses reassured them`,
"Absolutely not! My Lord is certainly with me—He will
guide me")**

When the army of Pharaoh closed in on the Children of Israel
and panic began to spread, Prophet Moses displayed
unwavering faith and absolute confidence in Allah's promise
of aid. While others faltered in fear and despair, Prophet
Moses remained steadfast, trusting in the mercy and power of
his Lord. His victory was not just a result of physical
strength, but of spiritual certainty in Allah's promise that
sustained him through that ordeal. In the face of
overwhelming trauma and danger, his faith became a beacon
of hope and a source of healing for his people.

*What are three ways you continue to think well of your Lord
and trust His promises, even when others around you lose
hope?*

231. Never Ask for Punishment

Chapter 26, Verse 187 (So cause ˹deadly˺ pieces of the sky to fall upon us)

Those whose hearts are sealed will not believe, even if shown every convincing sign. Their spiritual blindness is a barrier that no evidence can break. It is foolish and dangerous to challenge Allah's wisdom or to ask for punishment out of despair or frustration. For a believer, the path is clear: to seek forgiveness, to ask for Allah's pleasure, and to hold onto hope, even in the darkest moments of trauma and hardship. Healing begins with turning to Allah with humility and patience, rather than giving in to anger or hopelessness.

Have you truly done your best today to seek Allah's forgiveness and pleasure?

232. The Worst Ending

Chapter 26, Verse 227 (The wrongdoers will come to know what ˈevilˈ end they will meet)

Allah promises repeatedly in the Quran that the oppressed will ultimately prevail, while the oppressors will face humiliation and defeat. The gravest fate awaits those who inflict harm and injustice upon others—such cruelty leaves deep wounds not only on the victims but also on the oppressors' own souls. As believers, we are called to avoid that miserable end by dedicating ourselves to actions that build, heal, and restore justice.

Even in the face of overwhelming trauma and systemic oppression, our commitment to righteousness can be a powerful form of resistance and healing, for ourselves, our communities, and the Ummah.

What fears, doubts, or barriers hold you back from standing up for just causes around you?

233. Repair Ruptures

Chapter 27, Verse 11 (But if they later mend 'their' evil 'ways' with good)

There are those who commit the most distasteful and harmful actions, yet they see nothing wrong with their behavior. They twist the truth, concocting excuses and justifications to defend their wrongdoing. For such hardened hearts, hope may seem distant, and the wounds they cause run deep, often leaving survivors trapped in cycles of pain and mistrust. Yet, Islam never condones despair. No matter how far someone has fallen, every soul deserves a second chance—a path toward redemption and healing. This truth offers hope not only to the wrongdoers but also to those who have been hurt by them, reminding us that change is always possible.

How can you protect your heart from heedlessness, especially when faced with pain or betrayal?

234. The Dangers of Arrogance

Chapter 27, Verse 14 (And, although their hearts were convinced the signs were true, they still denied them wrongfully and arrogantly)

There are many who, out of arrogance and pride, deny the truth even though deep down they know with certainty that it is indeed the truth. This deliberate rejection not only corrupts their hearts but also prolongs suffering, both for themselves and for those affected by their denial. The ultimate end of such corrupt and stubborn souls is a grievous one, marked by loss and regret.

Denying truth, especially when it relates to justice or healing from trauma, can trap a person in cycles of harm and spiritual blindness. It also deepens wounds for victims who seek recognition and accountability.

How can you guard yourself from defending falsehood once the truth has been revealed to you?

235. Never Abuse Your Power

Chapter 27, Verse 34 (Indeed, when kings invade a land, they ruin it)

Most people, when given positions of power, unfortunately fall into the trap of abuse, corruption, and injustice, causing deep wounds and trauma to those under their authority. Such betrayal of trust can shatter communities and leave lasting scars on the oppressed. However, a true believer remains steadfast, holding onto high moral and ethical standards regardless of external pressures or circumstances. Even in the face of hardship, they do not compromise their integrity or lose their compassion.

Think of three people who have used their power wisely and compassionately to bring about good.

236. Believers are Strangers

Chapter 27, Verse 56 (But his people's only response was to say, "Expel Lot's followers from your land! They are a people who wish to remain chaste!")

Prophet Lot was casted out simply because he refused to engage in the vile sins that his people sought to impose upon him. His steadfastness in the face of such hostility led to alienation and rejection.

Sometimes, when people abandon or isolate you, it may be a sign that you are walking the right and righteous path, one that challenges corrupt norms and unjust pressures. Even the Prophets, the best of creation, have faced cruelty and harm from those blinded by arrogance and wrongdoing. Feeling alone, alienated, or like a stranger in your own community can be deeply painful and traumatic, yet liberating when your values and faith set you apart.

Have you experienced moments of loneliness, rejection, or estrangement because of your beliefs or principles? How do you interpret these experiences as signs of true faith?

237. Caring for the Prophet

Chapter 27, Verse 70 (Do not grieve for them, nor be distressed by their schemes)

Allah repeatedly reminds His beloved Prophet throughout the Quran to take care of himself and not to grieve over those who reject the message. Despite being chosen for this immense responsibility, the Prophet was deeply human; he felt pain, sorrow, and loneliness like any of us. One of his most profound qualities was his honest and consistent display of his human side, showing us that vulnerability and strength can coexist. He was so special because he was so human.

Reflect on the rejection and cruelty that Prophet Muhammad faced in Taif, the profound grief during the Year of Sorrow, and his miraculous journey to the heavens.

238. Feel Safe

Chapter 27, Verse 87 (And all those in the heavens and all those on the earth will be horrified except those Allah wills to spare)

Every one of Allah's creation will rise from their graves in fear, except for the few chosen ones whom Allah has granted peace and safety. Allah promises protection to those who endure adversity with unwavering faith throughout their painful and often traumatic journeys. Tyrants and oppressors should tremble at the thought of standing before Allah on that Day, for their reckoning will be severe and just. For the believer, true safety comes not from worldly power, but from steadfastness, sincerity, and trust in Allah amid trials.

How are you actively working to ensure your safety and peace on the Day when everyone else will be filled with fear?

239. Be an Inspiration

Chapter 28, Verse 5 (But it was Our Will to favor those who were oppressed in the land, making them models ˹of faith˺)

Allah promises that the oppressed will rise to become the leaders and inherit the earth after Allah removes the oppressors and their evil from the world. This Divine promise offers hope to those weighed down by trauma and injustice. However, when victims of trauma are finally given agency over their stories and lives, it is essential that they use this newfound power to heal their wounds and rebuild, rather than to inflict harm or perpetuate cycles of violence.

True leadership, especially born from hardship, requires wisdom, compassion, and strength rooted in mercy, not vengeance or cruelty. The journey from trauma to leadership is also a journey of transformation and responsibility.

What are three characteristics of a good leader who heals rather than harms?

240. Tend to Women's Hearts

Chapter 28, Verse 13 (So that her heart would be put at ease, and not grieve)

Allah returned Prophet Moses to his mother very quickly because He does not like mothers to grieve or be heartbroken.

Trauma leaves deep imprints, not only on the body and mind, but also on the heart and soul. We "keep the score" by releasing harmful stress hormones that affect our overall well-being. Allah, in His infinite mercy, desires to soothe and heal His female servants after trauma, just as He provided Mary with a detailed healing prescription while she endured the immense stress of conceiving Prophet Jesus. Allah does not wish for women to carry sadness or despair. Healing the hearts of women is a sacred responsibility, especially those closest to us.

What are three ways you can nurture and comfort the hearts of your female relatives—starting with your mother, wife, daughter, and sister?

241. Correct Mistakes

Chapter 28, Verse 17 (My Lord! For all Your favors upon me, I will never side with the wicked)

We are humans, and we all make mistakes. Sometimes, we may fall into the sin of siding with injustice, whether knowingly or unknowingly. Such actions not only harm others but also leave deep wounds on our own hearts and conscience, contributing to spiritual and emotional trauma. The weight of guilt can be heavy, but Allah's mercy is vast. When we recognize our wrongdoing, immediate repentance is essential. However, true repentance must be accompanied by concrete actions: distancing ourselves from those who commit evil and actively working to oppose injustice.

Like in the story of Prophet Moses, healing from the trauma of sinning involves both spiritual repair and practical change. It requires courage to admit fault, seek forgiveness, and commit to walking a different path.

What steps can you take to correct your mistakes after falling into sin? How can you ensure your repentance is sincere and followed by meaningful actions?

242. Do Good without Motive

Chapter 28, Verse 24 (So he watered ˹their herd˺ for them, then withdrew to the shade)

When Prophet Moses helped the two women in need, he did not boast, brag, or ask for anything in return. Instead, after fulfilling their needs, he quietly withdrew to the shade of a tree and engaged in sincere supplication to Allah. This humble and selfless act teaches us that true service to others is not for recognition or reward from people, but for the sake of Allah alone.

In the context of trauma, acts of kindness can be deeply healing, not only for those who receive but also for those who give. However, when good deeds are done for the sake of credit, recognition, praise, or personal gain, they can become burdens that weigh on the heart, adding to emotional exhaustion and spiritual strain.

How can you emulate Prophet Moses' example by helping others without seeking recognition or asking for credit?

243. The Gift of Brotherhood

Chapter 28, Verse 35 (We will assist you with your brother)

Allah saw Prophet Moses in need of support, so He made his brother a Prophet as well.

After experiencing trauma, one of the greatest blessings is having the unwavering support of immediate family, especially siblings who can stand by you through hardship and healing. Trauma can isolate a person, but the strength found in family bonds can provide a much-needed light during the darkest times. When we face trials, having someone who understands and supports us without judgment can be a lifeline.

Just as Allah granted Prophet Moses the companionship and aid of his brother Aaron, we too need to nurture those close relationships to help us endure and recover.

What are three ways you can actively strengthen your bond with your siblings?

244. Do Not Blindly Follow

Chapter 28, Verse 39 (And so he and his soldiers behaved arrogantly in the land with no right, thinking they would never be returned to Us)

Tyrants lead their followers astray, dragging many into destruction alongside themselves. When the punishment befell the Pharaoh of Egypt, not only was he drowned, but his entire army perished with him. This serves as a powerful reminder that blindly following a leader who opposes the teachings of the Quran and Sunnah can bring devastating consequences, not only for the leader but also for those who place their trust in them. Blind allegiance to a tyrant can lead to spiritual loss, moral decay, and soul harm. It can cause individuals and entire communities to become complicit in injustice and oppression, deepening collective trauma and generational suffering.

What are three dangers of blindly following a leader who does not adhere to the Quran and Sunnah?

245. Sin is Its Own Punishment

Chapter 28, Verse 47 (If struck by an affliction for what their hands have done)

The worst kind of misguidance is following one's own desires blindly. When the heart is spiritually blind, it accumulates sin upon sin, each one deepening the darkness within. This cycle of wrongdoing becomes its own form of punishment, as sins weigh heavily on the soul and cloud one's ability to see the truth or find peace. Sin often leads to inner turmoil, guilt, and a broken connection with Allah, which can exacerbate spiritual trauma. The heart becomes burdened and trapped by sins, making healing and repentance more difficult.

How can a sin become its own punishment, trapping a person in a cycle of distance from their Creator?

246. Allah Warns First

Chapter 28, Verse 59 (Nor would We ever destroy a society unless its people persisted in wrongdoing)

Allah does not destroy a nation except when they engage in actions that deserve such destruction. However, when the condition of the Ummah becomes so dire, like it is today, our collective sins and wrongdoings can bring harm not only upon the wrongdoers but also upon the innocent among us. This collective suffering deepens trauma, spreading pain and injustice across communities, affecting even those who are not directly responsible. Understanding Allah's justice requires recognizing that trials and tests are often a reflection of our own choices and the consequences of turning away from the Divine guidance. Yet, Allah's justice comes with mercy; He tests us to bring us back to the straight path, to awaken our hearts, and to allow space for repentance and healing.

What is the true meaning of Allah's justice when trauma is widespread?

247. Inherit Paradise

Chapter 28, Verse 83 (That ˹eternal˺ Home in the Hereafter We reserve ˹only˺ for those who seek neither tyranny nor corruption on the earth)

The Hereafter is reserved for those who refrain from both arrogance and corruption.

The power and tyranny of oppressors may shake the hearts of many and cause despair, especially for those living under injustice. However, the true believer remains steadfast, knowing that Allah's power is eternal and unshakable, far greater than any worldly force.

What lessons can you draw from the story of Korah about the consequences of arrogance before Allah?

248. Tests that Elevate

Chapter 29, Verse 3 (We certainly tested those before them. And ˹in this way˺ Allah will clearly distinguish between those who are truthful and those who are liars)

It is Allah's decree that we go through trials and tribulations in this life. Some people pass these difficult tests by showing sincere submission and contentment with their Lord, finding peace even amid pain and suffering. Others, overwhelmed by hardship, may lose sight of their Creator, valuing worldly matters above their faith and turning away from religion. These trials are not meaningless; they serve as a test of character. How we respond to suffering determines our place in the hereafter, whether we earn great reward or face severe punishment.

For victims of trauma, understanding this Divine wisdom can be both challenging and a source of hope, reminding us that pain does not go unnoticed or unrewarded.

How do you respond when someone asks, "Why do bad things happen to good people?"

249. The Day of Regrets

Chapter 29, Verse 25 (But on the Day of Judgment you will disown and curse one another)

You may witness how brutal and united some nations become when they gather to oppose Islam and its followers. Yet, rest assured that on the Day of Judgment, those who collaborated in evil would turn against one another, exposing the falsehood of their alliance, but by then, it will be too late for repentance or reconciliation.

For victims of injustice, this serves as a reminder that evil, no matter how powerful it seems in this world, is ultimately doomed to collapse. However, the scars left behind, on individuals, families, and communities, can last a lifetime, making it even more important to seek justice and healing now, while we still have time.

What are some ways people come to regret their harmful actions when faced with the consequences of the Hereafter? How can awareness of this accountability help you navigate your choices today?

250. Lessons to Learn

Chapter 29, Verse 38 (Which must be clear to you ˹Meccans˺ from their ruins)

Allah recounts the stories of many nations who rejected the truth and consequently earned His wrath. He shares these accounts so that we may deeply reflect on their mistakes, learn from their suffering, and strive to avoid their miserable fate.

For those who have endured trauma, whether personal or collective, these stories serve not only as warnings but also as sources of healing. They remind us that even in the darkest of times, turning back to Allah with sincerity, patience, and faith can bring restoration and strength.

Using the stories of the Prophets mentioned throughout the Quran, how can you build a healing toolkit?

251. None Escapes Justice

Chapter 29, Verse 40 (So We seized each ʿpeopleʾ for their sin)

No one escapes Allah's justice. Not Korah with all his wealth, nor Pharaoh with all his might, nor Haman with all his power, and for sure not today's tyrants.

For those coping with grief and traumatic loss, these stories serve as powerful reminders that worldly power and material possessions offer no protection against Divine justice and the ultimate reckoning. They also teach us about the transient nature of this life and the importance of placing our trust in Allah alone always, but especially in times of suffering.

What three stories from the Quran can you share with people who are struggling with grief and trauma—stories that offer comfort?

252. The Art of Dialogue

Chapter 29, Verse 46 (Do not argue with the People of the Book unless gracefully)

Allah advises us to argue with others gracefully and with wisdom. Most people are inherently good, but trauma and pain can create invisible walls between us, causing misunderstandings and division. When we respond with fury or lash out in anger, we often react from a place of fear—fear that is frequently rooted in ignorance or unresolved trauma. Instead of reacting harshly, approaching conflict with curiosity and compassion can open the door to healing and understanding.

How do you engage with wisdom and grace during arguments, especially when trauma and fear may be fueling the tension and mistrust?

253. Religion of Unity

Chapter 30, Verse 32 (Like' those who have divided their faith and split into sects)

Allah commands us to unite, especially in matters of faith, rather than divide. Yet trauma often causes people to regress, pulling inward into isolated corners, fostering suspicion, and pointing fingers at one another. This fragmentation only deepens the wounds and slows healing. True healing and strength come from building bridges of understanding, compassion, and inclusion, starting within our own communities.

In your own small community, how can you actively promote unity and inclusion, resisting the isolating effects of division and exclusion?

254. Your Sins Can Harm Others

Chapter 30, Verse 41 (Corruption has spread on land and sea as a result of what people's hands have done)

Allah warns that corruption arises from the deeds that people themselves have earned. The danger of sin is that it does not remain isolated; it can unravel the very fabric of society, spreading harm and suffering far beyond the individual. This collective damage can expose an entire nation to Allah's wrath and deepen the wounds caused by trauma.

How might your own sins affect not only yourself but also your family, community, Ummah, and even future generations?

255. Get Revived

Chapter 30, Verse 50 (See then the impact of Allah's mercy: how He gives life to the earth after its death!)

Just as Allah sends down rain to revive the barren, lifeless land, the Quran descends as a healing rain that revives our dead hearts and nourishes our wounded and ailing souls, especially after the storms of trauma and hardship. In times of deep pain and suffering, the words of Allah bring comfort, hope, and renewal when everything else feels out of order.

What are three ways you nurture and revive your heart and soul, at times of ease and hardship?

256. What is Your Story?

Chapter 30, Verse 54 (It is Allah Who created you in a state of weakness)

Human beings go through many stages throughout their lives. Each phase can be seen as a chapter in the book of our existence. While we may not be the authors of every chapter, especially those marked by pain, loss, or trauma, we still have the power to reclaim our narrative, to make meaning from our struggles, and to find healing even when the pages are stained or torn.

Write your story. Then decide whether to share it with others, confide in Allah, or keep it close to your heart.

257. Engage Beauty

Chapter 31, Verse 11 (This is Allah's creation. Now show Me what those ˹gods˺ other than Him have created)

With all the beauty surrounding us, in the heavens and the earth, across land, sea, and air, how could anyone deny the existence and greatness of Allah?

Yet, trauma can distort our perception, causing us to see only darkness and ugliness in the world and in those around us. It can trap us in pain, making it hard to recognize the sources of light and joy that still exist. Healing from trauma requires us to believe that beauty can return and that life can be whole again.

How is beauty an essential part of your healing journey?

258. Infinite Knowledge

Chapter 31, Verse 27 (The Words of Allah would not be exhausted)

If every single tree were turned into a pen, and all the water on this earth became ink, they still would not be enough to write down the words of Allah—not even a drop in the vast ocean of His infinite knowledge.

Especially after trauma, when we struggle to understand the reasons behind our pain, it is easy to feel lost or question Allah's wisdom. But our human knowledge is limited, fragile, and often clouded by suffering. Allah's knowledge and wisdom, however, are boundless and perfect.

How can you cultivate humility and patience, acknowledging your human limits while trusting Allah's infinite wisdom?

259. We Control Nothing

Chapter 31, Verse 34 (And no soul knows in what land it will die)

Man is naturally prone to arrogance. We often behave as if we are in full control of our destiny, as if our efforts alone shape every outcome. But the reality is, we control nothing. True control belongs solely to Allah.

This can be especially difficult to accept after experiencing trauma, when the chaos and pain make us feel powerless or desperate to grasp any semblance of control. Yet, holding too tightly to control can deepen our suffering, creating anxiety and frustration when things do not go as we wish.

Knowing that Allah is the One who ultimately decides all of our affairs, even when life feels unpredictable and overwhelming, how can you learn to surrender and truly let go of the illusion of control?

260. Divine Standards

Chapter 32, Verse 7 (Who has perfected everything He created)

Allah's standards are vastly different from ours. He acts according to His perfect wisdom and will, doing what He wishes, when He wishes, and in the way He has decreed. From the very moment we are born until the day we meet Him, He is in complete control.

During times of trauma, it is common for us to struggle—sometimes bargaining, questioning, or even arguing with Allah based on our limited human understanding. This is a natural response to deep pain, but it can also deepen our suffering if we forget that the Divine wisdom far surpasses our perspective.

Are you holding Allah to your human standards when navigating your pain?

261. Unimaginable Reward

Chapter 32, Verse 17 (No soul can imagine what delights are kept in store for them)

Those who abandon arrogance and dedicate themselves sincerely to worshiping their Creator, while serving His creation, are promised a reward beyond human comprehension. The blessings Allah has prepared for them in Paradise exceed even their wildest imagination.

For those who have endured pain, loss, and trauma, the hope of such unimaginable peace and joy becomes a powerful source of healing. It reminds us that no matter how heavy our burdens, there is a promise of relief and eternal comfort waiting beyond this life.

What are you yearning for in Paradise?

262. A Blessed Ummah

Chapter 33, Verse 6 (The Prophet has a stronger affinity to the believers than they do themselves. And his wives are their mothers)

The wives of the Prophet are honored as the Mothers of the Believers, holding a special place of respect and guidance. The Prophet serves as a father figure for the entire Ummah, and is our source of comfort, strength, and wisdom.

In times of confusion, his life and teachings become our moral compass, guiding us through the chaos and uncertainty around us. His example teaches patience and compassion, showing us how to endure pain while remaining steadfast in faith.

Take time to learn three new things about the family of our beloved Prophet.

263. Prophets Are Human

Chapter 33, Verse 11 (Then and there the believers were put to the test, and were violently shaken)

Even the Prophet, the best of all creation, and his closest companions faced extremely difficult trials and moments that tested and shook their faith. Their challenges remind us that suffering and trauma are part of the human experience, even for the most righteous. What truly matters during such times of adversity is to remain steadfast on the right path, holding firmly to faith despite the heavy winds that try to shake or uproot us.

Trauma can deeply unsettle the soul and cause doubt to creep into even the strongest hearts. How can you anchor and ground your heart in the unshakable promise of Allah's ultimate aid?

264. Do Not Falter

Chapter 33, Verse 22 (The promise of Allah and His Messenger has come true)

A believer places unwavering trust in the promises of Allah and His Prophet. Indeed, what they promise is the ultimate truth, even when it does not bring immediate ease or relief.

Often, the path is filled with hardship and struggle. It is through these struggles—through enduring pain, trauma, and uncertainty, that the believers draw closer to Allah, who then guides them more firmly towards Himself. In times of widespread suffering and turmoil, especially given the current affairs of the Ummah, it can be difficult to hold onto hope. Yet, it is precisely in these dark moments that faith in the promise of ultimate victory and justice becomes a lifeline.

How can you continue to believe in the promise of victory despite the miserable affairs of the Ummah today?

265. Win Without Fighting

Chapter 33, Verse 25 (And Allah spared the believers from fighting)

Some victories require no fighting at all. When we place our complete trust and reliance in Allah, He can grant us triumph in ways beyond our imagination—often through patience, wisdom, and steadfast faith rather than winning a physical battle.

In times of trauma, it is easy to feel overwhelmed by the need to "fight" or resist in conventional ways. Yet, some of the most profound victories come from surrendering to Allah's plan, staying united and holding firm to faith despite the chaos.

What are some battles you can overcome without raising a sword or engaging in conflict?

266. The Choice is Allah's

Chapter 33, Verse 36 (It is not for a believing man or woman—when Allah and His Messenger decree a matter—to have any other choice in that matter)

It is not befitting for a believing man or woman to follow their own desires or personal opinions over the clear guidance of Allah and the Prophet. When Allah and the Prophet have already decided on a matter, our role is one of submission, trust, and obedience, even when it challenges our own feelings or understanding.

Trauma can cloud our judgment, making it tempting to rely on personal feelings or give in to doubts. But true healing and growth come from surrendering to Divine wisdom, especially when the path is difficult or unclear.

Before you form your next opinion or take a stance, ask yourself: Does it align with the guidance of Allah and the Prophet?

267. Do Not Hurt the Prophet

Chapter 33, Verse 53 (And it is not right for you to annoy the Messenger of Allah)

The beloved Prophet cares deeply for us, bearing the weight of our struggles and pain. The Ummah has no right to hurt him in any way, whether through neglect, disrespect, or turning away from his teachings. The least we can do is honor and respect our beloved Prophet by following his guidance and upholding his legacy, especially during times of trauma and hardship. When the Ummah strays, it adds to the Prophet's sorrow another wound upon a heart already burdened by the suffering of his people.

In what ways might the Ummah be causing pain to its beloved Prophet today?

268. Care for the Creation

Chapter 33, Verse 72 (But humanity assumed it)

Allah entrusted His creation with a heavy responsibility: to be the caretakers and stewards of this earth. Only mankind accepted this great burden, while the rest of creation recoiled, aware of the weight it carries. This trust is immense and requires patience, strength, and wisdom, especially in times of adversity, when the pain and suffering around us can feel overwhelming.

Name three things Allah has entrusted you with. Are you nurturing and protecting your responsibilities amidst the chaos?

269. Nothing is Hidden

Chapter 34, Verse 3 (Not 'even' an atom's weight is hidden from Him)

It is striking and heartbreaking how some people openly expose their sins and defiantly challenge their Creator, as if forgetting the consequences that await them.

The beloved Prophet taught us to feel sincere regret and remorse for our sins, but to never publicly expose our private faults, as this only deepens our spiritual wounds and opens us up to further harm.

In times of trauma, it can be especially difficult to maintain our commitment to Allah's rules. What Islamic teachings do you find most challenging to uphold during your struggles? How can you strengthen your resolve and seek healing through repentance and patience?

270. Reject Evil Invitations

Chapter 34, Verse 20 (Indeed, Iblîs' assumption about them has come true)

Most people easily accept invitations to evil, following their whims and desires without hesitation. The danger of instant gratification and indulging our lusts and desires is that it creates layers of separation between us and Allah, deepening the spiritual wounds trauma often leaves behind. When we chase fleeting pleasures, we lose sight of the healing and peace that come from closeness to our Creator. To improve our collective external situation, the state of our Ummah and the world, we must first commit to doing the difficult internal work of healing ourselves.

What are three evil invitations or temptations you have recently faced? Write them down, place them in an envelope, and then burn or shred it as a symbolic act of rejection and commitment to turning away from harmful paths.

271. Never Lower Your Standards

Chapter 34, Verse 25 (You will not be accountable for our misdeeds, nor will we be accountable for your deeds)

The Prophets and Messengers of Allah are the best of His creation. They engaged with their communities with grace and patience, even when slandered, insulted, or betrayed. Remaining graceful in the face of hatred is incredibly difficult, yet the Prophets showed us it is possible through unwavering faith and trust in Allah's wisdom. Their example teaches us how to carry the heavy burdens of pain and rejection without losing dignity and hope. A true believer always aims high, even when weighed down by the shackles of trauma.

Imagine drawing a well with a deep, full bottom. Then choose a spot at the top representing a goal or a vision to strive for.

272. Only You and Your Deeds

Chapter 34, Verse 37 (It is not your wealth or children that bring you closer to Us)

Neither our wealth nor our children will benefit us when we stand before Allah. In the face of tragedy, these worldly attachments can feel painfully fragile and fleeting. Only strong faith and sincere good deeds serve as the true path toward salvation and spiritual elevation. When everything else falls away, what remains are the fruits of our faith and actions.

What three things will follow you to your grave? Of those three, which one will stay with you?

273. Have Awe

Chapter 35, Verse 10 (To Him ʿalone˒ good words ascend, and righteous deeds are raised up by Him)

The goodness of our speech and the righteousness of our deeds ascend to our Lord.

In moments of trauma and hardship, our words and actions carry even greater weight. They can either heal wounds or deepen scars. Therefore, it is essential to choose our words and deeds with care.

What does Allah send your way and what do you send His way?

274. A Double-edged Sword

Chapter 35, Verse 28 (Only the knowledgeable 'of His might' are 'truly' in awe of Him)

Those who possess knowledge should be the most conscious and fearful of their Lord. Knowledge is a double-edged sword. Knowledge that does not draw you closer to Allah is not true or beneficial knowledge. It can become a source of pride, arrogance, or even harm.

This reality should deeply concern some religious and faith scholars who, despite their status, support tyrants and deviant leaders, causing harm to the oppressed and distorting the truth.

In times of trauma and injustice, the role of knowledge is even more critical. It must guide us toward healing, compassion, and justice, not division or corruption.

Is the knowledge you hold bringing you closer to Allah, or is it leading you away from Him and the path of righteousness?

275. Everything is Written

Chapter 36, Verse 12 (Everything is listed by Us in a perfect Record)

Allah knows everything you send forth to your hereafter and everything you leave behind on this earth long after you are gone. Every action, no matter how small or hidden, is recorded, and will be accounted for.

In the midst of trauma and hardship, it can be easy to lose track of our deeds or feel overwhelmed by our mistakes. Yet, it is precisely during these times that self-reflection and accountability become most crucial for healing and growth.

At the end of today, take a moment to write down all the deeds you engaged in, both the good and the bad. Express deep gratitude for the good deeds, and feel sincere remorse for the shortcomings.

276. Standing before Allah

Chapter 36, Verse 53 (It will only take one Blast, then at once they will all be brought before Us)

We should deeply reflect on the reality that, with just one command from our Lord, all of His creation, from the beginning of time until its very end, will stand before Him on the Day of Judgment.

In moments of trauma, when the weight of suffering feels unbearable, remembering this ultimate accountability can offer both comfort and hope. Allah is just and never wrongs His creation; every hardship, every trial, every act of patience and faith is recorded with perfect justice. What we find waiting for us in the bank of our hereafter will be exactly what we have deposited through our intentions and actions in this life.

Take time to research and reflect on the seven categories of people who will be granted shade under Allah's throne on the Day of Judgment.

277. Own Witness

Chapter 36, Verse 65 (On this Day We will seal their mouths)

On the Day of Judgment, mouths will be sealed shut, and it will be our hands, feet, and all parts of our bodies that will bear witness to our deeds. This reality should deeply humble and even frighten us, especially when we consider the grave consequences for those who caused harm and showed no mercy to Allah's creation.

Trauma often leaves invisible scars, but on that day, every action, whether born from kindness or cruelty, will be laid bare. Those who inflicted pain without compassion will face a horrifying fate, their bodies testifying against them for the suffering they caused.

Take a moment to list the organs and limbs of your body. Reflect on how each part can be a means of healing and goodness, rather than harm.

278. Glorious is Allah

Chapter 36, Verse 82 (All it takes, when He wills something ˹to be˺, is simply to say to it: "Be!" And it is!)

When Allah wills something to happen, He simply says "Be," and it comes into existence.

In moments when every door seems to slam shut, and we feel trapped with no options left, we must hold onto the unwavering certainty that Allah can change our circumstances in the blink of an eye.

Trauma often makes us feel powerless and stuck in the darkness of depression, but Allah's power to transform even the bleakest situations is limitless.

Reflect deeply on the three most difficult challenges you are currently facing. Lay them sincerely before Allah, trusting in His mercy and ability.

279. Think Good About Allah

Chapter 37, Verse 87 (What then do you expect from the Lord of all worlds?)

One of the most powerful acts of worship that is often overlooked is thinking well of Allah. This is not easy, especially when we are engulfed in pain, and suffering that cloud our hearts and minds. Yet, it remains a vital tool for healing that we must strive to master.

When trauma shakes our faith and fills us with doubt or despair, choosing to trust in Allah's wisdom, mercy, and justice can bring profound peace and strength.

What does it truly mean to think good about Allah, especially when your heart is burdened with pain?

280. Victory is a Guarantee

Chapter 37, Verse 173 (And that Our forces will certainly prevail)

Allah has promised that His army will be victorious. True victory comes when we fulfill the conditions He has set, through patience, steadfastness, faith, and righteous action.

In times of hardship and trauma, when despair tries to weaken us, remembering this promise can be a source of hope and strength. Victory is not always immediate or visible to our standards, but it is assured for those who remain sincere and committed despite the challenges.

How are you ensuring victory for the Ummah?

281. Be a Lifeline

Chapter 38, Verse 17 (And remember Our servant, David, the man of strength)

Allah described Prophet David as having many hands, even though he only had two. This is because his impact and dedication to serving Allah's creation were felt everywhere. His hands were multiplied through his sincere efforts and devotion.

In times of trauma and hardship, when we feel powerless or broken, we can find inspiration in how Prophet David's unwavering commitment created ripples of healing and goodness that reached far beyond himself.

Look around at the good projects happening in your community. How can you contribute?

282. Be Attuned

Chapter 38, Verse 28 (Or should We treat those who believe and do good like those who make mischief throughout the land?)

Those who build and those who destroy are never equal. Allah loves those who heal wounds, not those who inflict pain and suffering.

In a world where trauma can leave deep scars on individuals and communities alike, choosing to be a source of healing is a powerful act of faith.

Have you taken a step today to heal a wound, to ease someone's pain, or to bring peace rather than harm?

283. Avoid Disgrace

Chapter 38, Verse 60 (No! You are not welcome!)

On the Day of Judgment, the people of Hellfire will see one another and be filled with regret and sorrow. They will exchange blame and supplicate against each other, overwhelmed by the weight of their punishment. The worst fate is reserved for the oppressors, those who inflicted pain, injustice, and trauma on others in this life. Their end is a grave warning to all of us.

Reflect deeply on the honor bestowed upon the people of Paradise, contrasted with the disgrace and torment of those in Hell.

284. Hold On To Hope

Chapter 39, Verse 36 (Is Allah not sufficient for His servant?)

When everyone else walks away, remember that you always have Allah by your side.

In moments of deep loneliness and pain, when the world seems to abandon you, how can you truly feel alone knowing that Allah's presence never leaves?

Who do you truly count on for support when life's burdens feel too heavy to bear?

285. Choose Your Fate

Chapter 39, Verse 47 (they will see from Allah what they had never expected)

On the Day of Judgment, those who have committed injustice will witness realities far beyond what they ever imagined—realities that fill them with regret and despair. But by then, their late remorse will bring them no relief or mercy.

Can you imagine the weight of the worst punishment, where the pain of their evil actions finally catches up to them? Tyrants, who caused suffering and oppression in this world, will face severe consequences.

Can you feel Allah's ultimate justice before you see it with your own eyes?

286. The Verse of Hope

Chapter 39, Verse 53 (Say, 'O Prophet', that Allah says "O My servants who have exceeded the limits against your souls! Do not lose hope in Allah's mercy")

Many scholars consider this to be the most hopeful Verse in the Quran. We are truly a blessed Ummah to have Allah, The Most Merciful, The Compassionate, as our Lord and Sustainer.

In the midst of trauma, loss, and hardship, holding onto this hope becomes a lifeline that nurtures our wounded hearts and strengthens our spirits. Allah's mercy is infinite, even when the world around us lacks mercy.

How do you keep hope alive during these trying times?

287. Walk into Paradise

Chapter 39, Verse 73 (When they arrive at its ˥already˥ open gates)

Allah vividly describes how the Hellfire opens its doors, raging with anger at its inhabitants, while Paradise warmly and joyfully welcomes those who are deserving of its eternal pleasures. This stark contrast reminds us of the consequences of our actions and the realities that await us.

For those burdened by trauma, these images serve as a powerful call to seek healing.

Reflect deeply on how Paradise and Hell receive their dwellers—with mercy and joy on one hand, and with wrath on the other.

288. When Voices Are Silenced

Chapter 40, Verse 16 (Who does all authority belong to this Day?)

On the Day of Judgment, the tyrants will be silenced, powerless before the voice of Allah, the King of kings and the Lord of Majesty and Might. In this ultimate moment of truth, all will submit to His judgment, and no worldly power will protect those who caused harm and injustice.

Knowing that your tongue has the power to heal or to wound deeply, how can you learn to control it with compassion and wisdom?

289. Tyrants Mislead Followers

Chapter 40, Verse 29 (Pharaoh assured 'his people', "I am telling you only what I believe, and I am leading you only to the way of guidance")

Like the Pharaoh of Egypt, many tyrants throughout history, and even today, murder and oppress people for no other reason than their faith in Allah and their refusal to bow to falsehood. They commit horrific crimes and then justify their actions with twisted logic, propaganda, or fear. But on the Day of Judgment, blaming others, following orders, or claiming ignorance will not be a valid excuse. Each soul will be held accountable for its choices, silence, and complicity.

Trauma often makes people freeze, disconnect, or feel helpless in the face of injustice. Healing requires reclaiming your agency and choosing to stand with the oppressed, even in small, consistent ways.

In all your actions, public or private, online or offline, how can you make sure you are not following, enabling, or justifying any form of oppression?

290. Oppression Seals Hearts

Chapter 40, Verse 35 (This is how Allah seals the heart of every arrogant tyrant)

When Pharaoh arrogantly declared himself a lord worthy of worship and dared to challenge Allah, his end was nothing short of catastrophic. His story is a timeless warning about what happens when power is abused and delusions of grandeur replace humility before the Creator. Oppression not only harms others, it severs the oppressor's connection to Allah. It hardens the heart, blinds the soul, and ultimately bars the servant from Divine mercy.

Trauma survivors, especially those who have experienced tyranny or injustice, may find deep validation in this story. It reminds us that unchecked power and cruelty do not go unnoticed by Allah and that Divine justice will prevail, even if it is delayed.

What inner qualities led to Pharaoh's downfall? How can you ensure you never adopt even traces of these qualities, especially when given authority or influence?

291. Allah is Listening

Chapter 40, Verse 60 (Your Lord has proclaimed, "Call upon Me, I will respond to you")

What gives us hope, even in our darkest moments, is Allah's promise that He responds to every sincere supplication.

For those who have been silenced, ignored, or dismissed, this promise is a lifeline.

Do you remember a time when you felt that no one heard you? How did it feel to pour your heart out to Allah?

292. Ultimately, Allah Decides

Chapter 40, Verse 77 (Whether We show you some of what We threaten them with, or cause you to die ˹before that˼, to Us they will ˹all˼ be returned)

Allah commanded His beloved Prophet to be patient, for the promise of Allah is coming without a doubt. Some Prophets were blessed to witness victory in their lifetimes, while others returned to their Lord before seeing the fulfillment of that promise. Yet none of them was forgotten. In Allah's hands lie all wise and ultimate decisions.

For those who carry the wounds of disappointment, who have waited for justice, healing, or change for so long, this is not easy to accept. Trauma often makes time feel frozen. It tells us that if relief has not come yet, it might never come. It whispers lies that patience is weakness and that hope is naïve. But Allah sees what you cannot. He knows what your heart has endured and how long it has waited. He delays with wisdom. He withholds with love. His timing is not a denial, it is a preparation.

The next time you feel defeated, tired, or overlooked...Can you accept that Allah, in His infinite wisdom, decides the terms, the timing, and the end of this painful chapter?

293. Late Regrets Mean Nothing

Chapter 40, Verse 85 (But their faith was of no benefit to them when they saw Our torment)

Many will spend their lives in heedlessness and corruption. Only when they see the punishment of Allah or come face-to-face with the truth will they begin to plead, saying they now wish to repent. But when the Divine decree arrives and when Allah's anger descends upon a people, it may be too late to change.

Sometimes trauma tricks us into believing that we have time. That we can delay our healing. That the damage we are doing to ourselves or others is not that serious. But every moment spent in sin, in injustice, or in neglect of our hearts is a moment further away from the light of Allah. Sin does not just distance you from Allah. It delays your healing. We ask for victory on personal, communal, and global levels, but victory requires preparation. One of the fastest ways to prepare for victory is to leave behind the very sins that block it.

What would it look like to live with a mindset of constant repentance? Not out of shame, but out of love. Not because you fear punishment, but because you long to be close to your Lord.

294. Enemies into Friends

Chapter 41, Verse 34 (Respond ˹to evil˺ with what is best, then the one you are in a feud with will be like a close friend)

Good and bad deeds are never equal. Even when you are hurting, it is still better to respond with grace. Why? Because you never know what someone is carrying — the burdens they are hiding, the wounds they have never healed from, or the pain that shaped their behavior. Sometimes the people who hurt us the most are operating from their own unresolved trauma. Responding to them with harshness might only deepen their defensiveness. But when you respond with mercy, patience, and dignity — even to those who are hostile — you may soften a heart that no one else could reach. Allah tells us that grace can turn enemies into intimate friends. That is not idealism, it is Allah's word.

What can change people's hearts? Know that grace is one of the most powerful change-makers.

295. Guidance and Healing

Chapter 41, Verse 44 (It is a guide and a healing to the believers)

The original title of this book was "Guidance and Healing". That title still holds true. Because one of the most powerful tools for healing trauma, especially deep emotional and spiritual wounds, is spending time with the words of Allah. Not just reading them, but sitting with them, letting them speak to your pain, letting them hold your heart. Allah is the ultimate Healer. And He did not just send down rules, He sent down relief, comfort, meaning, and mercy through the Quran.

For hearts weighed down by grief, for minds exhausted by confusion, and for souls carrying invisible scars, the Quran is a Divine pharmacy. It is not just a book of theology or law. It is healing for the seen and the unseen.

Why did Allah refer to the Quran as the ultimate source of healing?

296. Walk Towards Allah

Chapter 41, Verse 51 (And when touched with evil, they make endless prayers ˹for good')

Most people are ungrateful. In times of hardship, they run desperately toward Allah, seeking His help, His mercy, and His intervention. But when the storm passes and life feels calm again, they often walk away. They forget. They distance themselves from the very source of their healing. This cycle is all too human, especially for those living with trauma. Pain forces us to our knees, sometimes in desperation. But ease can bring a false sense of control, as if we no longer need the One who sustained us. Yet, the true believer, the one who has tasted both despair and Divine rescue, stays near. They remain by their Master's door, in hardship and in ease, because they have learned not to trust the illusion of stability. They have learned that the One who carried them through the fire is the only One worth clinging to in the calm.

Most people walk away from Allah in times of ease. How can you walk toward Him, not just in pain, but also in joy?

297. Make a Decision

Chapter 42, Verse 7 (A group will be in Paradise and another in the Blaze)

It would have been easy for Allah to guide all of His creation with a single command. But in His perfect wisdom, He gave us something powerful, the ability to choose. With choice comes accountability. With decisions come consequences, both in this life and the next. Sometimes, our choices are shaped by fear. Sometimes, we act from survival rather than clarity or faith. And still, Allah sees it all: the brokenness, the effort, and the struggle.

Healing is also a choice. But it is not always a straightforward or easy one. To heal is to confront your demons and hidden skeletons, to challenge old beliefs, to sit with pain you have long tried to avoid. Healing is a choice that often has to be made again and again, each morning, each prayer, each time you fall and get back up again. And Allah is gentle with those who try. He guides those who want to be guided. He heals those who reach out for healing, even if all they can offer is a broken whisper.

Do you believe that man has free will? Is healing a choice?

298. Worth Striving For

Chapter 42, Verse 20 (Whoever desires the harvest of the Hereafter, We will increase their harvest)

If you strive for the Hereafter, Allah will guide you to the best of both this life and the next. But if you strive only for this life, you may receive your share here and be left with nothing there. This life is temporary. But when you are hurting, grieving, or simply trying to survive after trauma, it is easy to get caught in the urgency of now — the need to feel better right now, to escape pain right now, to prove yourself right now. That is human. But it is also why Allah lovingly reminds us, again and again, to lift our gaze. To anchor our hearts not in temporary outcomes, but in eternal truths. True healing begins when we re-center the Hereafter as our priority and when we ask ourselves: Is this choice bringing me closer to Allah or further away? Allah knows your pain. He knows how trauma skews your priorities, numbs your purpose, and clouds your clarity. But still, He calls you, patiently and consistently to something higher and more lasting.

What is on your current priority list?

299. The Choice to Forgive

Chapter 42, Verse 43 (And whoever endures patiently and forgives—surely this is a resolve to aspire to)

Allah gave permission to the oppressed to fight for justice; and when they achieve victory, it becomes their choice to practice the virtue of forgiveness. Forgiveness is not weakness; it is a powerful, conscious choice and a virtue that reflects inner strength. It does not erase the trauma or pain, but it frees the heart from the burden of hatred, resentment, and holding grudges. Healing, too, is a choice. It is a journey that often requires us to move beyond waiting for apologies or acknowledgment from others. You can begin to heal even if those who caused your pain never seek forgiveness or make amends. This truth can be difficult for those carrying the wounds of trauma: healing is your path, and it starts within you. Your abuser does not have to write the next chapter of your story.

What does forgiveness mean to you in the context of your own healing? How can you choose healing today, even if those who hurt you are not part of that journey?

300. Dismantle Toxic Structures

Chapter 43, Verse 22 (In fact, they say, "We found our forefathers following a way, and we are following in their footsteps")

Many people blindly follow the traditions and ways of their ancestors without questioning them. However, Islam calls us to break free from toxic cultural shackles that may trap us in patterns of pain, injustice, and stagnation.

Trauma can often be passed down through generations, hidden within cultural norms and unspoken rules that prevent healing and growth. If your cultural baggage is hindering your healing, whether through harmful beliefs, silence around trauma, or oppressive practices, it is vital to seek authentic sources of healing rooted in the Quran and Sunnah. True healing requires courage to challenge what no longer serves you and to embrace what brings peace and restoration to your heart and soul.

How is your culture influencing your healing journey, either positively or negatively?

301. Wishful Thinking

Chapter 43, Verse 78 (But most of you were resentful of the truth)

The criminals, lost in their delusions, will cling to all kinds of wishful thinking—hoping for mercy or reprieve, but none of it will benefit them when they face the full wrath of Allah. In that moment of ultimate reckoning, they will plead and beg Allah for even a brief respite from punishment, yet their prayers will go unanswered. This is a painful reality for those who have caused harm and injustice in this life, failing to tame their souls or seek true repentance. Trauma inflicted on others will echo back, and the weight of unatoned sins will crush the heart in the hereafter. One way to avoid all of that tomorrow is to stop hurting people today.

Reflect on the unfulfilled wishes and desperate pleas of those who lived unjustly on the Day of Judgment.

302. Some Are Never Missed

Chapter 44, Verse 29 (Neither heaven nor earth wept over them)

Neither the heavens nor the earth will shed tears for the criminals who caused harm and injustice. However, the tears and blood of the oppressed will never be in vain; they are engraved in the record of justice, witnessed by Allah, and will be answered in the hereafter.

Trauma inflicted by oppression leaves deep wounds, not only on individuals, but also on entire communities and generations. Yet, Allah promises that He does not forget the suffering of the oppressed, and their patience and pain will be honored with ultimate justice.

How will people remember you after your death? Will your legacy be one of compassion and healing, or one marked by harm and evil?

303. Allah as Your Guardian

Chapter 45, Verse 19 (Allah is the Patron of the righteous)

Tyrants and criminals often unite, supporting each other in their injustice and oppression, spreading fear and trauma among the innocent. Meanwhile, Allah supports and strengthens those who sincerely lean on Him, especially in times of hardship and persecution.

The collective trauma inflicted by oppressive regimes can fracture communities, instill despair, and sow division. Yet, Allah's support brings hope to the faithful, reminding them that true strength comes from reliance on Him alone.

Consider the Prophet's saying that nations will gather against Islam.

304. Do Not Be Forgotten

Chapter 45, Verse 34 (It will be said, "This Day We will neglect you as you neglected the meeting of this Day of yours!")

On the Day of Judgment, Allah will turn away from those who intentionally turned away from Him in this life. Those who neglected their connection with their Creator, often lost in worldly distractions, risk being excluded from Allah's mercy.

Trauma and hardship can sometimes cause people to feel abandoned or to distance themselves from Allah out of despair or confusion. Yet, it is precisely during these times that holding onto faith and seeking Allah's remembrance becomes most crucial for healing and salvation.

What steps are you taking today to keep your heart connected to Allah, ensuring you are not among those forgotten?

305. Rest in Paradise

Chapter 46, Verse 14 (It is they who will be the residents of Paradise, staying there forever, as a reward for what they used to do)

Allah commands us to strive and work hard in this life, for true and eternal rest is not found here, but is reserved for the hereafter.

Life's trials, hardships, and trauma can wear us down, making the idea of rest feel distant and unreachable. Yet, it is through persistent effort, patience, and faith that we prepare ourselves for the ultimate peace and rest promised in Paradise.

What are you working hard on today to earn the eternal rest and tranquility of Paradise?

306. Arrogance Blinds

Chapter 46, Verse 26 (But neither their hearing, sight, nor intellect were of any benefit to them whatsoever, since they persisted in denying Allah's signs)

Many nations became so consumed by their own desires and arrogance that they failed to recognize the signs of punishment approaching them. Their blindness was not just physical but spiritual—a result of sins that darkened their hearts and prevented them from seeing the truth of their eventual standing before Allah.

Trauma, whether personal or collective, can deepen this blindness, making it harder to face reality or seek repentance. When a heart is burdened with sins, it becomes numb, disconnected from the mercy and warnings of its Lord.

What are some sins that blind a person from turning back to Allah?

307. A Divine Gift

Chapter 46, Verse 35 (So endure patiently, as did the Messengers of Firm Resolve)

When the tribes around Makkah rejected the Prophet, turning away from his message and subjecting him to hardship and isolation, Allah did not leave him alone in his pain. Instead, He caused other parts of His creation—angels, jinn, and believers from distant lands, to listen to the Prophet's message and believe in it. In the midst of rejection and heartbreak, Allah surrounded the Prophet with unseen support and strengthened his spirit, showing that even when human hearts turn away, the Divine support remains steadfast.

What did Allah do to heal and mend the Prophet's broken heart during times of rejection? How do you appreciate Allah's most precious gift of guidance?

308. Give Victory to Allah

Chapter 47, Verse 7 (O believers! If you stand up for Allah, He will help you and make your steps firm)

Allah promised that true victory belongs to those who grant Him victory through their sincere obedience and steadfastness.

In times of trauma and hardship, when the path feels uncertain and the weight of struggle is heavy, it is our obedience to Allah that becomes the means to invite His support and triumph. Though Allah is the ultimate source of victory, He empowers us to be active partners in achieving it by submitting our will to His guidance and commands.

How can you give victory to Allah when He is the source of victory?

309. The Hour is Here

Chapter 47, Verse 18 (Yet ˹some of˺ its signs have already come)

The signs of the Hour are upon us, yet many remain blind to them, overwhelmed by the chaos surrounding them.

Trauma can cloud our vision, making it difficult to recognize the clear signs that point to the approaching Day of Judgment. Amidst the confusion and pain, it is crucial to awaken our hearts and minds to these signs, so we may prepare ourselves for what is to come. Recognizing the signs is not meant to instill fear and anxiety, but to inspire readiness, reflection, and sincere repentance.

Take time to research the signs of the Hour. How can you prepare yourself and your loved ones to face these realities with faith?

310. Corruption Breaks Families Apart

Chapter 47, Verse 22 (Now if you ˹hypocrites˺ turn away, perhaps you would then spread corruption throughout the land and sever your ˹ties of˺ kinship!)

Allah warns strongly against corruption and severing the ties of kinship, for such actions tear apart the very fabric of our communities.

Trauma, when left unaddressed within families, can deepen these wounds and create painful divides. Yet one of the greatest strengths a family can have is to confront their trauma together, standing united through compassion, patience, and forgiveness. In times of hardship, healing becomes a collective journey—mending broken bonds, restoring trust, and embracing one another despite past hurts. This unity not only eases individual pain but protects the family from falling into further discord.

Look closely at your relationships with your relatives. Where are the ruptures caused by trauma? How can you take the courageous steps to repair and rebuild those ties?

311. Show Dignity

Chapter 47, Verse 35 (So, do not falter)

The believers carry dignity in their hearts. Even in the face of hardship, they do not display weakness or humiliation, for they hold firm the certainty that Allah is always with them—supporting, uplifting, and protecting them. This inner strength is born from faith, not pride. True dignity is a shield against the wounds of trauma; it allows believers to stand tall with humility and grace, without slipping into arrogance or harshness. It is the quiet confidence that comes from trusting in Allah's plan, even when life's trials threaten to overwhelm.

What does it truly mean to embody dignity without crossing that line into arrogance?

312. Hold Your Post

Chapter 48, Verse 4 (To Allah ˹alone˺ belong the forces of the heavens and the earth)

Allah described signing the treaty, not taking over the city of Makkah, as a clear sign of victory. His wisdom and plans often unfold in ways beyond our understanding. Allah works in mysterious ways. He has the power to do whatever He wills, whenever He wills, and His timing is perfect, even when we feel lost or overwhelmed by waiting for relief.

In moments of confusion or despair, it can be difficult to trust the unseen path Allah has set. But sometimes, what feels like a setback is actually part of a greater plan that we cannot yet comprehend.

Is it better to be at the tail of a caravan moving in the right direction, or to be at the head of a caravan moving the wrong way?

313. Do Not Break Your Pledge

Chapter 48, Verse 10 (Whoever breaks their pledge, it will only be to their own loss)

When you make a pledge, remember that your promise is first and foremost made with Allah, even before the person standing before you. Breaking a pledge is not just a betrayal of trust with others, but a betrayal of your covenant with Allah Himself.

In times of trauma and hardship, when your spirit feels fractured and your resolve weak, holding fast to your promises can be one of the hardest tests. Yet, it is in these moments that faith and integrity shine through.

What promises have you made to Allah?

314. How is Your Heart?

Chapter 48, Verse 18 (He knew what was in their hearts, so He sent down serenity upon them)

When Allah saw the sincerity, purity, and deep belief in the hearts of the Prophet's companions, He granted them victory. It was not their numbers, wealth, or weapons that made the difference, rather the state of their hearts. Victory, in this life and the next, often begins in the unseen realm of the heart.

In the journey of healing, too, the heart plays a central role. Trauma does not just impact the body or mind—it weighs heavily on the heart and the soul. A wounded heart can feel overwhelmed, guarded, numb, or even disconnected. But with faith, compassion, and intention, even the most shattered heart can begin to mend.

Draw and paint a heart. How is your heart holding all this pain?

315. Submit, for Victory

Chapter 48, Verse 27 (Indeed, Allah will fulfill His Messenger's vision in all truth)

When the Prophet and the believing men and women around him fully submitted to the will of Allah, despite the pain, loss, and setbacks they endured, Allah rewarded them with a victorious return to their homeland. That victory was not just physical—it was spiritual, emotional, and a deeply healing experience. The Prophet was no stranger to trauma. He was born into loss, losing many loved ones throughout his blessed life. He knew the sting of abandonment, the ache of grief, and the isolation of being rejected by his own people. And yet, he remained steadfast, patient, and trusting in Allah's promise.

Take a moment to reflect on the many tragedies the beloved Prophet experienced, not just as a messenger, but also as a human being.

316. Listen When Allah Speaks

Chapter 49, Verse 1 (Do not proceed ˹in any matter˺ before ˹a decree from˺ Allah and His Messenger)

The Prophet and his companions embodied deep humility when interacting with fellow believers, offering compassion, gentleness, and support especially to those who were struggling. Yet, when faced with those who were actively hostile toward Islam and committed to spreading harm, they stood with unwavering strength, clarity, and dignity. This balanced emotional posture—softness for the wounded and firmness with the wounding, is not always easy, especially for those who have been traumatized. Trauma can confuse our boundaries. We may become overly guarded with those who mean us well, and too forgiving with those who harm us. But Allah reminds us that discernment is key. When Allah speaks, the believer listens—not selectively, but wholeheartedly.

How do you show humility toward fellow believers, especially those who are different from you or going through their own trials? And how do you maintain your dignity and clarity when facing people or systems that are unjust or oppressive?

317. Collaborate, Do Not Compete

Chapter 49, Verse 13 (And made you into peoples and tribes so that you may ˹get to˺ know one another)

Allah created us into different nations and tribes so that we may know one another—not to divide, destroy, or hate, but to build, collaborate, and grow through mutual understanding and shared humanity. Diversity was never meant to be a source of conflict. It is a Divine gift and a means of healing, not harming. Yet trauma, especially collective trauma across generations or communities, can make us suspicious of others' intentions. It can create barriers where bridges should be. Sometimes, when we see someone else working on a healing project or building something good, our own pain and unhealed wounds may cause us to feel threatened or envious, rather than inspired. But healing is not a competition. It is a shared journey. Supporting others in their work, especially when it is aligned with our values, is part of our own healing too.

Given the many wounds and unmet needs in your community and beyond, what are some ways you can support, rather than undermine, the healing projects led by others?

318. Tyrants Should Feel Terrified

Chapter 50, Verse 14 (Each rejected ˈtheirˈ messenger, so My warning was fulfilled)

Allah, who destroyed entire nations in the past for their arrogance, oppression, and transgression, is fully capable of doing the same to the tyrants of today. His justice may be delayed, but it is never denied.

For those who have lived through, or are still living under, oppressive systems, it can feel terrifying and even dangerous to speak the truth or challenge injustice. Trauma can silence the tongue and shake the heart. Fear becomes embedded not just in the mind, but in the body, making safety feel unreachable. And yet, standing up for truth is not always about confrontation. It is about integrity and resistance, even in quiet ways. It is about finding safe and strategic ways to speak, to act, to support others, and to protect the vulnerable without endangering yourself in the process.

How can you safely and wisely stand up in the face of tyranny or injustice?

319. Allah is Near

Chapter 50, Verse 16 (And We are closer to them than ˹their˺ jugular vein)

Allah is closer to you than your own jugular vein. When your heart longs to speak to Him, enter into prayer. When your soul yearns to hear His voice, open His Book. Every Verse is a message meant just for you.

In moments of deep loneliness, when the world feels distant, and people seem unavailable or unsafe, remember: Allah has never left your side. He is not only near—you are held, seen, and known by Him in ways no one else can understand.

For those carrying unhealed wounds, the feeling of being abandoned or invisible can run deep. Trauma often tells us we are alone, even when we are surrounded by people. But Allah, in His mercy, reminds us: "I am near". Not only physically, but intimately.

How does your heart respond to knowing that Allah is near—even in your lowest, messiest, and most lonely moments?

320. Look Within

Chapter 51, Verse 21 (As there are within yourselves. Can you not see?)

We are commanded to reflect on the signs of Allah, not just in the vastness of the heavens and the intricacies of the earth, but especially within our own creation. The human body is among the greatest miracles—a perfectly designed system, sustained moment by moment by Allah's mercy. Look outward to witness the majesty of Allah's creation. Look inward to recognize His presence in your very being.

For those who carry trauma in their bodies, this reflection can be difficult. When pain, fear, guilt, or shame has been stored in our genetics, it can be hard to view the body as sacred or a place of Divine beauty. But Allah, in His wisdom, did not make a mistake in creating you. Every breath you take, every heartbeat, every cell that regenerates is a testimony to Divine care, even if your body has carried wounds, betrayal, violation, or silence.

How can you begin to see your body not only as a container of pain, but as a reflection of Divine love? Keep reminding yourself: I am worthy of contemplation. I am worthy of healing.

321. Run Towards Safety

Chapter 51, Verse 50 (Flee to Allah!)

In times of deep distress, we are not meant to run away—we are meant to run towards. With Allah is the ultimate refuge, the source of safety, stability, and comfort when the world feels unsteady or threatening.

When fear overtakes the heart, and uncertainty clouds the mind, it is only in the remembrance of Allah that we can truly find comfort.

Reflect on the moment when the Prophet and Abu Bakr hid in the cave during their migration. What might it look like to turn to Allah in the exact moment of feeling overwhelmed?

322. The Purpose of Creation

Chapter 51, Verse 56 (I did not create jinn and humans except to worship Me)

Allah tells us that the very reason for our creation is to worship Him. But worship is not limited to mechanical acts or lifeless rituals. True worship is a living connection—a way of being that includes our acts of worship, yes, but also our service to others, our acts of kindness, our coping through pain, and our choices in the face of hardship.

What is the purpose behind your creation? Are you living a life that is aligned with that purpose?

323. Eternal Reunion

Chapter 52, Verse 21 (As for those who believe and whose descendants follow them in faith, We will elevate their descendants to their rank)

Allah promises in the Quran that those who believe, and whose children or descendants follow them in faith, will be reunited together in Paradise, even if they were at different levels.

This is one of the most hopeful Verses for anyone who has tasted the pain of separation, whether through loss, distance, or difficult relationships. When trauma enters a family, it can leave behind not just emotional scars, but also spiritual disconnection. Generational pain, misunderstandings, and emotional neglect can damage the very relationships we pray to preserve in the next life. But Allah, in His mercy, reminds us that faith can heal and reunite, not only in this world but in the next. Even if families were broken in this life, they can be mended in Paradise, if all hold onto belief and strive for righteousness.

What steps are you currently taking to guide your family toward faith, healing, and emotional safety and ensure your ultimate reunion in Paradise?

324. Under Allah's Very Eyes

Chapter 52, Verse 48 (So be patient with your Lord's decree, for you are truly under Our ˹watchful˺ Eyes)

Allah commanded His beloved Prophet to be patient, assuring him that he is under the direct protection of His Lord. Imagine the profound sense of safety and peace that comes from knowing you are guarded by Allah Himself, especially when the world feels chaotic, overwhelming, or hostile.

For those who have endured trauma, feeling truly safe can seem impossible. But Allah's protection is unlike any worldly security; it is a shield that no harm can penetrate, a sanctuary where the heart can find refuge in the middle of the storm.

What does it truly mean to be under Allah's watchful eyes? In your most vulnerable moments, do you sense that Divine presence?

325. Be Careful What You Wish For

Chapter 53, Verse 24 (Or should every person ˈsimplyˈ have whatever ˈintercessorsˈ they desire?)

If a person were able to get everything they wished for every single time, it would still be only a temporary gain compared to the eternal blessings that Allah has prepared.

In moments of trauma and loss, it is natural to yearn for relief, justice, or restoration. Yet, worldly wishes, no matter how deeply desired, can never fully heal the wounds of the soul or replace what is truly lasting in Allah's eternal mercy and reward.

What do you wish for most deeply right now? Are your wishes aligned with what pleases Allah?

326. Healing Possibilities

Chapter 53, Verse 58 (None but Allah can disclose it)

With Allah, healing is always possible. Even if healing comes late, it is better than never healing at all. Healing is not only a possibility—it is also a responsibility entrusted to us by our Creator.

Trauma can leave deep wounds that feel impossible to mend, and sometimes the pain can seem endless. Yet, Allah's mercy is vast, and He encourages us to seek restoration and wholeness, no matter how broken we feel. Healing may take time, patience, and effort, but it is never beyond reach when we place our trust in Him, our Ultimate Healer.

Regardless of how deep or painful your trauma is, do you truly believe that healing is possible?

327. A Difficult Day

Chapter 54, Verse 8 (The disbelievers will cry, "This is a difficult Day!")

When the disbelievers rise from their graves and gather for questioning on the Day of Judgment, they will be overwhelmed with regret for every wrong they committed in this fleeting life. That day will be unbearably heavy—a day of reckoning unlike any other. In the depths of their regret, they will realize how the choices they ignored or the chances they wasted have led them to a painful and irreversible fate. The weight of that moment will be crushing, as they face the consequences of their deeds with no opportunity to turn back.

How can you begin to rectify the regrets you hold today, before it is too late?

328. No One Defeats Allah's Army

Chapter 54, Verse 45 ('Soon' their united front will be defeated and 'forced to' flee)

When the arrogant gather to oppose the believers and challenge Allah, He promises that no matter how big or powerful their armies may be, they will ultimately face defeat. Their pride blinds them to the reality that true power belongs only to Allah, and arrogance only leads to destruction. The higher someone rises in arrogance, the more devastating and painful their fall becomes. This fall is not just physical but spiritual—a shattering of false pride that leaves them broken, exposed, and stripped of all false security.

How do the stories of the arrogant, like the army that planned to destroy the house of Allah with their elephants, remind you of the dangers of pride in your own life?

329. Allah is in Command

Chapter 54, Verse 50 (Our command is but a single word, done in the blink of an eye)

Everything, no matter how big or small, is precisely preordained by Allah. Every moment, every event, every hardship and joy, unfolds according to His Divine wisdom and decree. When Allah is truly in control, what reason is there to fear His creation, which is limited and fleeting?

In the midst of trauma, pain, and uncertainty, it can be easy to feel overwhelmed or abandoned. But remembering that Allah governs all things with perfect knowledge and mercy brings a deep sense of peace and security, even when the world feels chaotic and unjust.

How does knowing that Allah controls everything affect your response to trauma?

330. Only Allah Remains

Chapter 55, Verse 27 (Only your Lord Himself, full of Majesty and Honor, will remain ˹forever˺)

Everything and everyone, no matter how powerful or mighty, will inevitably perish, except for Allah, the Praiseworthy, the Lord of Magnificence and Honor.

This reality can be deeply unsettling, especially when we face loss, betrayal, or trauma that shakes the very foundation of our lives. The impermanence of all creation reminds us that the pain we endure, as overwhelming as it feels, is temporary. Yet, it also calls us to reflect on where we place our trust and hope.

How does the inevitability of death and loss impact your perspective on the trauma you have experienced?

331. Come Back Home

Chapter 57, Verse 16 (Has the time not yet come for believers' hearts to be humbled at the remembrance of Allah and what has been revealed of the truth)

Allah commands us to show Him true humility, for humility is the healing balm for hearts that have grown hard and burdened by pain.

Trauma, grief, and life's hardships can cause the heart to become closed off, distant, and resistant. Yet, through sincere humility before Allah, recognizing our need for His mercy and guidance, we begin to soften and heal from the inside out.

In what ways has trauma or hardship affected the state of your heart? What are three practical steps you are taking to tame and soften your heart in the face of pain?

332. Be Pleased with Allah

Chapter 57, Verse 22 (No calamity 'or blessing' occurs on earth or in yourselves without being written in a Record before We bring it into being)

Whatever tests and tribulations we endure have already been decreed by Allah's Divine wisdom and knowledge. These challenges, though often painful and overwhelming, are part of a greater plan that we may not fully comprehend in this life. In the face of trauma and hardship, our greatest strength lies in surrendering with full submission to Allah's will and finding contentment in His decisions, even when our hearts ache and our wounds bleed. Acceptance does not mean passivity; it means trusting that every trial carries a purpose—whether it is to purify, teach, or elevate us, and that Allah's mercy encompasses even our deepest wounds.

How are you working to cultivate a heart that is pleased with Allah's decree even after adversity?

333. Allah Tells the Truth

Chapter 58, Verse 21 (Allah has decreed, "I and My messengers will certainly prevail")

In a world filled with deception and hidden agendas, many seek to harm the faith and its followers, plotting in darkness against Islam and its people. Yet, despite their schemes and cruelty, Allah and His faithful army will ultimately be victorious. This promise is certain and unbreakable.

The wounds inflicted by those who oppose the truth can leave deep scars, fracturing communities, sowing doubt, and shaking faith. In such times of spiritual and emotional trauma, it is crucial to remain vigilant about who and what we support, as our choices either strengthen the Ummah or contribute to its demise.

What criteria do you use to discern who and what deserves your support and loyalty?

334. Give, Even When in Need

Chapter 59, Verse 9 (They give 'the emigrants' preference over themselves, even though they may be in need)

Some give generously for the sake of Allah, even when they have barely enough for themselves. This selflessness becomes most evident when you visit refugee camps and war zones—places marked by loss, suffering, and broken dreams. In the face of unimaginable hardship and trauma, these people still open their hearts and hands to others. They embody the spirit of the people of Madinah, who gave everything they had to support their brothers and sisters who migrated from Makkah, despite their own struggles. Such generosity is not charity; it is a profound act of healing through altruism.

The next time you find yourself in need; can you gather the strength to give instead of receiving?

335. Cowardly Enemies

Chapter 59, Verse 14 (You think they are united, yet their hearts are divided)

The enemies of Islam encourage one another to disobedience and wrongdoing, but when the punishment of Allah befalls them, they quickly turn to blame and accuse each other. Their true nature is revealed—they are cowards. They never confront their opponents openly or face consequences directly. This cowardice deepens the wounds of the Ummah, as these enemies sow division, fear, and suffering from the shadows, rather than standing boldly and accepting accountability.

Name three examples that reveal how cowardly the enemies of Allah truly are.

336. Do Not Trust Allah's Enemies

Chapter 60, Verse 1 (O believers! Do not take My enemies and yours as trusted allies)

A true believer must never befriend the enemies of Islam, for those who do risk falling into misguidance and straying from the straight path.

In times filled with betrayal and deception, the line between friend and foe can become blurred, deepening the wounds of the heart and weakening the Ummah from within. Trust becomes precious and fragile, easily shattered by false alliances and hidden agendas.

In these days of widespread betrayal and hardship, who can you truly trust with your heart and faith? How do you protect yourself and your community from those who seek to mislead and harm, from outside and from within?

337. A Successful Trade

Chapter 61, Verse 10 (O believers! Shall I guide you to an exchange that will save you from a painful punishment?)

The best transaction you can ever make is with Allah. When you trade with Him, offering your sincere faith, patience, and righteous deeds, you gain the priceless reward of Paradise in return. Yet, in the trials and turmoil of life, it is easy to lose sight of this ultimate exchange, distracted by fleeting worldly gains that leave the heart wounded and restless.

When you see an opportunity to trade with Allah, to invest your time, energy, or wealth for His pleasure, do you seize it with hope and conviction?

338. A Beneficial Knowledge

Chapter 62, Verse 5 (The example of those who were entrusted with ˹observing˺ the Torah but failed to do so, is that of a donkey carrying books)

Those who receive Allah's message but then turn away from it are in grave danger. They neglect to transform that precious knowledge into meaningful action, leaving their hearts vulnerable to despair, confusion, and spiritual ruin. Ignoring guidance not only wastes the blessing of knowledge, but also deepens the wounds of the soul, pulling one further from healing and mercy.

Have you ever experienced a moment when, despite pain or hardship, you acted on even the smallest piece of knowledge? How did that choice impact your journey toward healing and closeness to Allah?

339. Spend

Chapter 63, Verse 9 (Do not let your wealth or your children divert you from the remembrance of Allah)

Many people will wish that their death is delayed or that they could return to life after death, just so they could dedicate more time and effort in the cause of Allah. This deep yearning comes from the painful realization that life is fleeting and that the opportunity to do good will eventually end, sometimes abruptly, leaving hearts heavy with regret and unfulfilled purpose.

How can you spend in the cause of Allah today, before it is too late?

340. Divine Promise

Chapter 65, Verse 7 (Allah does not require of any soul beyond what He has given it. After hardship, Allah will bring about ease)

Allah said that no matter how ugly our circumstances or how severe our trauma, ease after hardship is a Divine promise.

Can you live a life centered on Allah, expecting nothing but beauty in whatever He decrees?

341. Treating Combatants

Chapter 66, Verse 9 (O Prophet! Struggle against the disbelievers and the hypocrites, and be firm with them)

Allah commanded the Prophet to fight against the disbelievers and the hypocrites—those who actively and persistently plot against Islam, and to show harshness toward them, not mercy. This stern approach was necessary to protect the community from ongoing harm and betrayal. It is crucial to understand the distinction between how to treat combatants who pose a direct threat, and civilians who are innocent and should be protected from harm.

Imagine the trauma inflicted on a community by constant betrayal and hostility from those who undermine faith and safety. The Prophet's command to show firmness toward such enemies reflects the reality of protecting a vulnerable society from destruction. Yet, this firmness must be balanced with justice and mercy toward the innocents caught in the turmoil.

How do you differentiate between standing firm against oppression and ensuring mercy toward those not involved?

342. Grace Facing Death

Chapter 67, Verse 2 (˹He is the One˺ Who created death and life in order to test which of you is best in deeds)

One way to cope with death and life's difficulties is through grace—an act of profound strength and patience.

It is not easy to remain graceful in the face of loss, pain, and uncertainty, yet it is a Divine quality exemplified by the Prophets. Their grace amid suffering teaches us that even in the darkest moments, dignity and trust in Allah's wisdom can provide healing. Consider how death, one of the most painful and inevitable experiences, can shake the soul to its core. Trauma from loss often brings grief, anger, and despair. Yet, the ability to show grace amid such trials does not mean suppressing pain, but rather embracing it with patience and faith. This grace becomes a source of healing, allowing wounds to slowly mend and the heart to find peace.

How can you cultivate grace when facing the heavy weight of death and loss?

343. The Best Role Model

Chapter 68, Verse 4 (And you are truly ˹a man˺ of outstanding character)

When Allah described His beloved Prophet, He emphasized his perfect manners, ethics, etiquettes, and flawless character. Despite facing immense hardship, relentless persecution, and deep personal loss, the Prophet remained a beacon of compassion, patience, and unwavering integrity.

In the midst of trauma and suffering, it can be difficult to hold onto hope or emulate such noble qualities. Yet, the Prophet's example shows us that even in the darkest times, one can embody grace. His character was a source of healing, not only for himself but also for an entire Ummah struggling with pain.

What qualities of the noble Prophet draw you closer to him?

344. Standing for Questioning

Chapter 70, Verse 4 (on a Day fifty thousand years in length)

The Day of Judgment equals fifty thousand years, a time when every action, word, and thought will be unveiled before Allah. Nothing—no secret, no hidden deed, will escape His knowledge. Imagine standing for fifty thousand years, facing the weight of every moment of your life laid bare. The trauma of regret, fear, and accountability will be overwhelming for those unprepared. This is a day when excuses vanish and the reality of our deeds confronts us with full clarity.

What have you done to prepare yourself for standing for questioning before Allah?

345. Respect Allah's House

Chapter 72, Verse 18 (The places of worship are ˹only˺ for Allah, so do not invoke anyone besides Him)

The house of Allah belongs to Him alone, and it must be a sanctuary and a place of absolute safety, peace, and sincere devotion.

Yet, in a world filled with turmoil, fear, and brokenness, many masjids stand silent, disconnected from the healing and refuge they are meant to provide. Imagine the pain of those seeking comfort and finding empty walls instead of open hearts. The trauma of loneliness, fear, and despair deepens when sacred spaces meant for healing and community feel distant or lifeless. Our local masjid should be a refuge where wounds are tended to, hope is restored, and faith is strengthened.

What steps can you take to bring your local masjid to life, turning it into a true haven of safety and healing?

346. Care, Within Reason

Chapter 74, Verse 44 (Nor did we feed the poor)

When the people of the Hellfire are asked why they earned its eternal torment, they respond by admitting that, besides neglecting their prayers and doubting the inevitable return to Allah, they failed to care for the needy. Instead, they wasted their lives chasing empty, meaningless pursuits while the cries of the vulnerable went unheard.

Imagine the deep regret and despair of realizing, too late, that a life spent ignoring the suffering around you leads to eternal loss. The trauma of wasted time, lost opportunities, and ignored responsibilities weighs heavily on the soul when faced with the stark reality of the Hereafter.

How do you find balance serving the needs of others and fulfilling your duties without allowing yourself to be overwhelmed or burned out by the weight of the world's pain?

347. Only Escape Towards Allah

Chapter 75, Verse 10 (On that Day one will cry, "Where is the escape?")

One stage of the soul's journey is to become deeply remorseful, feeling the weight of blame for having engaged in actions that displease Allah. This remorse often pierces the heart like a wound, shaking the very core of our being, as we confront the pain of our mistakes and the fear of Allah's displeasure. True remorse is not just regret; it is a soul's painful awakening to its own shortcomings, a profound acknowledgment of the damage caused both to oneself and to the relationship with the Divine and the creation. This inner turmoil can feel overwhelming, but it is a necessary step towards healing and returning to Allah's mercy.

Research the criteria for sincere remorse.

348. For Allah's Sake

Chapter 76, Verse 9 (Saying to themselves,` "We feed you only for the sake of Allah, seeking neither reward nor thanks from you")

On the Day of Judgment, believers who enter Paradise will be honored by Allah Himself. Imagine the overwhelming awe and relief in that moment, after enduring the trials of this life and the terrors of the Hereafter, to receive such blessings from the Most Merciful. This promise should awaken a deep hope within our hearts amid the darkness of our struggles and the pain of our past.

When faced with the trauma and the fear of the final reckoning, these hopeful deeds become beacons of light and reminders that Allah's mercy is vast and His reward is beyond measure.

What are the deeds you hold onto most dearly, the ones that give you hope for inheriting Paradise despite the weight of your sins and trials?

349. Ultimate Justice

Chapter 78, Verse 18 (ʿit isʾ the Day the Trumpet will be blown, and you will ʾallʾ come forth in crowds)

Whatever you do in this life, whether good or bad, will be accounted for and rewarded or punished in the Hereafter. Allah's judgment is perfect and absolute; there will be no injustice on that Day, no matter how hidden or ignored injustice seemed in this world.

For those who have suffered deeply, the promise of Allah's flawless justice is a lifeline amid the chaos. When earthly systems fail and cruelty goes unanswered, the Day of Judgment assures that every tear, every wound, and every unjust act will be fully recognized and balanced.

How can the certainty of Allah's ultimate justice bring comfort and hope to the oppressed, whose pain is often ignored or dismissed in this life?

350. Restrain Your Soul

Chapter 79, Verse 40 (And as for those who were in awe of standing before their Lord and restrained themselves from 'evil' desires)

For those who truly fear Allah's majesty and are constantly aware of His watchful gaze upon them, those who restrain their souls and control their desires, the promise is Paradise.

In a world full of temptations, pain, and confusion, controlling the restless soul can feel like an endless battle, especially when trauma shakes our inner peace. Yet, it is through this struggle—this conscious restraint, that healing begins and the soul is refined. Restraining the self is not just about discipline; it is about protecting your heart from further wounds and nurturing it toward hope and salvation.

What are some ways you actively restrain and refine your soul?

351. No Worldly Protection

Chapter 80, Verse 37 (For then everyone will have enough concern of their own)

On the Day of Judgment, people will even turn away from their own families, overwhelmed by the weight of their own deeds and fears. Everyone will be consumed by their own struggles, leaving no one to rely on but themselves.

In times of deep trauma and crisis, we often discover how fragile human support can be. When everything collapses and those closest to us are unable or unwilling to help, who will truly stand by our side?

Write a list of people you believe can help you. Now, think again—where does your true support lie?

352. We Have All We Need

Chapter 81, Verse 28 (To whoever of you wills to take the Straight Way)

The Quran is a clear and shining roadmap for those lost and seeking guidance amid life's storms. In its Verses, we find not only direction but also the healing balm for our deepest wounds.

When trauma and confusion cloud our hearts, the Quran remains our moral compass, showing us the way toward peace, hope, and restoration.

Engage with the Quran every day, especially when your soul feels fractured and weary. Make it a daily refuge.

353. Never Challenge Allah

Chapter 82, Verse 6 (O humanity! What has emboldened you against your Lord, the Most Generous?)

What causes a person to stand defiantly against their Lord? Humans, in their frailty, can become deeply arrogant and ungrateful, turning away from the very source of their sustenance.

In moments of pain, confusion, or trauma, some may challenge Allah's wisdom, forgetting that their trials are tests meant to bring them closer to Him. Others may let arrogance blind their hearts, leading them to disobey despite knowing the weight of accountability that awaits them.

What are some ways people rebel against their Lord even when they know the consequences?

354. The Greatest Loss

Chapter 83, Verse 15 (Undoubtedly, they will be sealed off from their Lord on that Day)

The greatest torment is to be denied the ultimate blessing—the chance to gaze upon the Face of Allah. To be veiled from this Divine beauty is the most devastating loss, a fate far worse than any worldly suffering. Imagine the deep despair and regret of those who, after a lifetime of choices, find themselves cut off from this eternal light.

How can you protect yourself from such a heart-wrenching fate? What steps are you taking today to nurture your soul and earn the honor of Allah's nearness?

355. Avoid Questioning

Chapter 84, Verse 8 (They will have an easy reckoning)

The people of Paradise will face an easy and gentle questioning before Allah, after which they will joyfully reunite with their families in eternal bliss.

Imagine the relief and peace that comes after the harsh trials of this life, finally followed by this moment of Divine mercy.

What can you do today to prepare your heart and actions so that you may avoid a difficult reckoning altogether?

356. Die for Allah

Chapter 85, Verse 8 (who they resented for no reason other than belief in Allah—the Almighty, the Praiseworthy)

Throughout history, tyrants have oppressed those who stand against their cruel and twisted ideologies, silencing truth with violence and fear.

The pain and suffering of the oppressed often go unseen by the world, yet Allah's justice is always near.

Reflect deeply on the story of the people of the trench.

357. Invest in the Hereafter

Chapter 88, Verse 9 ('Fully' pleased with their striving)

On the Day of Judgment, some faces will be darkened by shame and humiliation, weighed down by the burden of their deeds, while others will shine bright with dignity and peace, reflecting the rewards of their actions in this life.

The Day of Judgment will unveil every hidden pain, every injustice suffered, and every soul's true state.

What steps are you taking today to earn the light of honor rather than the shadow of regret tomorrow?

358. Mind Allah

Chapter 89, Verse 23 (This is when every ˹disbelieving˺ person will remember ˹their own sins˺. But what is the use of remembering then?)

When the son of Adam stands before Allah, and the angels and the blazing Hellfire is brought before him, he will be overwhelmed by regret for all the wrongs he committed in this life. Every missed opportunity, every neglected duty, will weigh heavily on his heart—yet at that moment, none of his remorse or pleas will benefit him.

Can you commit to doing good frequently and consistently, before it is too late?

359. Go as High or as Low

Chapter 91, Verse 8 (Then with ˹the knowledge of˺ right and wrong inspired it!)

We are granted free will — a powerful gift but also a heavy responsibility. We can choose to indulge in fleeting desires that corrupt our pure, innate nature, leading us away from the path of righteousness. Or, we can summon the strength to resist those temptations, even when the world around us pulls us in every direction, and strive instead to be among the elite who remain steadfast.

In a world full of chaos, pain, and relentless pressure, how can you stay true to your core values and protect the purity of your soul?

360. Our Prophet, Our Blessing

Chapter 93, Verse 5 (And ˹surely˺ your Lord will give so much to you that you will be pleased)

One of the most hopeful Verses in the Quran is the promise Allah made to His beloved Prophet that he will be pleased on the Day of Judgment. Yet, the Prophet will find true joy only when his entire Ummah is granted entry into Paradise.

Imagine the weight of this hope amidst the trials, loss, and suffering faced by the believers throughout history—the promise of ultimate mercy and reunion in the hereafter with our beloved.

Which Verses in the Quran ignite deep hope in your heart?

361. Prostrate to Heal

Chapter 96, Verse 19 (Continue to˙ prostrate and draw near ˙to Allah)

The closest moment to your Lord is when you humbly prostrate before Him. In that vulnerable position, you are completely exposed—your pain, your fears, your deepest struggles laid bare. Spend intimate time with Allah in prostration. Complain to Him, pour out your heart, and share your story, no matter how incoherent it feels.

Make a prayer mat. Turn a corner in your house into a sacred space where you can return again and again to find solace, healing, and closeness to Allah amidst life's trials.

362. Questioned About Everything

Chapter 99, Verse 6 (On that Day people will proceed in separate groups to be shown the consequences of their deeds)

On the Day of Judgment, even the smallest of our good and bad deeds will be brought to light. Nothing, no matter how hidden or seemingly insignificant, will escape Allah's perfect justice.

In this life, take time to count your blessings with sincere gratitude, especially when trauma and hardship threaten to overshadow your heart. Gratitude is a shield that softens pain and nurtures healing.

Be mindful to avoid indulgence and extravagance in a world where many suffer.

363. Giving and Getting Advice

Chapter 103, Verse 3 (And urge each other to the truth, and urge each other to perseverance)

Humanity is at a loss—lost in confusion, pain, and despair, except for those who believe, perform righteous deeds, and consistently encourage one another to uphold truthfulness and patience amid trials.

In the face of trauma and hardship, having a strong support network can be a lifeline—a circle of trusted souls who listen, advise, and uplift when burdens feel unbearable.

How can you begin building a network of sincere and compassionate people to turn to in moments of struggle and uncertainty?

364. Join Allah's Army

Chapter 110, Verse 1 (When Allah's ultimate help comes)

The victory of Allah is certain and inevitable, with or without our participation. Yet, one of the greatest honors and sources of healing for the wounded soul is to join Allah's victorious army by striving to reach our full potential, through sincere worship and selfless service.

In a world scarred by pain and injustice, how can you rise above your struggles and become one of Allah's soldiers who help bring about true and lasting victory?

365. The Only Refuge

Chapter 114, Verse 1 (I seek refuge in the Lord of humankind)

Our only true refuge lies with Allah. He is the shelter that protects us from the unseen and visible evils that surround us, especially after the deep wounds trauma leaves behind.

In moments of despair and fear, Allah's protection is the anchor that holds us steady when everything else feels shaky.

What are three sources of refuge you turn to after trauma? Is the shade of Allah your safest refuge?

CONCLUSION

The 365 tools mentioned in this book are only a small glimpse of what the Quran offers when it comes to healing the invisible wounds of trauma. This is intended to be "a Divine guide", not "the Divine Guide". It is my humble contribution toward finding meaningful solutions to the deep issues that trouble our world. It also reflects my personal interpretation of some of the timeless messages that Allah has sent to all of us. I am sure I will have made mistakes in the process, and for that, I ask for your grace and forgiveness.

The trauma of loss is one that heavily affects the Muslim Ummah. The loss of our beloved Prophet was the greatest calamity the Ummah has ever endured. He himself experienced countless trials, more than anyone could bear. He was the most tested man in history, and still, he remained merciful, patient, and beautiful in character. His example is a living roadmap for anyone striving to process pain, live with purpose, and be a source of healing.

Among the difficulties our beloved faced are the following:

• Death of his father, Abdullah – before the Prophet was even born.

• Death of his mother, Aminah – when the Prophet was only six.

Growing up as an orphan made the Prophet care deeply about the orphans and the emotional needs of the youth around him.

- Death of his grandfather, Abdul-Muttalib – when the Prophet was eight.

- Verbal abuse, mockery, and social boycott.

Receiving insults did not tempt him to retaliate or lower his standards. He treated even his enemies with grace.

- Torture and persecution of his followers, and the killing of many of them.

Witnessing trauma made him attuned to those struck by grief. He was always in the company of the forgotten.

- The loss of his beloved wife Khadijah and his uncle Abu Talib in the same year "The Year of Sorrow".

Losing his most reliable supporters made him lean on Allah alone for refuge and protection, while at the same time encouraging us to build strong social support networks around us.

- Three-year economic and social boycott, leading to starvation.

Going through famine made him look after the invisible needs of his Ummah. He did not eat or sleep before people felt safe and cared for.

- Physical attacks and assassination attempts.

- Forced migration to Medina (Hijrah).

Going through the refugee experience, he had a soft spot in his heart for those forcibly displaced.

- Participation in battles.

He led with courage, but never glorified war. He wept for the fallen and prayed even for the "enemy". He ordered mercy towards the civilians and prisoners of war.

- Loss of six out of seven of his children. Also some of his grandchildren.

To lose even one child is one of the most painful experiences a parent can go through. Imagine losing six. Yet, he cried openly, teaching us that grief is not a weakness. He said, "The eyes shed tears, the heart grieves, but we do not say anything except that which pleases our Lord".

- Insults to his honor and character assassination.

He did not lash out. Rather, his character spoke louder than their slander.

- Betrayals by tribes, hypocrites, and some People of the Book.

Despite being deeply hurt, he upheld justice and continued to treat people with fairness.

- Personal health struggles in his final years:

He bore physical pain with patience, constantly turning to Allah and increasing his worship.

And finally, he was always worried about his Ummah. The day he left the world, his heart was longing to meet us. The feelings are mutual, we love you too our dear Prophet.

The Prophet was not just a Messenger. He was a healer. He lived through loss, betrayal, poverty, grief, violence, and rejection, yet remained anchored in love, faith, and service.

If we truly love him, we must also embrace him as someone who knew suffering deeply and turned it into mercy for all creation. His emotional intelligence is a timeless lesson for our own healing journeys.

I would like to conclude this book with one of my favorite supplications, found in **Chapter 46, Verse 15: "My Lord! Inspire me to ˈalwaysˋ be thankful for Your favors which You blessed me and my parents with, and to do good deeds that please You. And instill righteousness in my offspring. I truly repent to You, and I truly submit ˈto Your Willˋ"**.

May Allah include us among His elite who He described in **Chapter 33, Verse 23: "Among the believers are men (and women) who have been true to their covenant with Allah"**.

May Allah make this effort a source of guidance, healing, and blessings. May He accept it sincerely for His sake. May we strive to live with sincerity, excellence, and grace, and may we be worthy of the company of the Prophet in the highest Paradise.

Thank you for taking this journey with me. May Allah bless you and your loved ones. Please remember me and my family in your prayers. May Allah be pleased with us all and may we meet in Paradise.

www.ingramcontent.com/pod-product-compliance
Lightning Source LLC
Chambersburg PA
CBHW061550120626
46550CB00004B/1440